CANDID REFLECTIONS:

Letters from Women in Architecture 1972 & 2004

OTHER BOOKS BY DORIS COLE

- *School Treasures: Architecture of Historic Boston Schools*
  with Nick Wheeler, Photographer

- *The Lady Architects: Lois Lilly Howe, Eleanor Manning
  and Mary Almy, 1893–1937*
  with Karen Cord Taylor

- *Eleanor Raymond, Architect*

- *From Tipi to Skyscraper: A History of Women in
  Architecture*

CANDID REFLECTIONS:

Letters from Women in Architecture 1972 & 2004

Doris Cole

Midmarch Arts Press
New York

Library of Congress Control Number 2006940159
ISBN 978-1-877675-63-8

Printed in the United States of America

Published by
Midmarch Arts Press
New York, NY 10025

CONTENTS

ACKNOWLEDGMENTS

This book is an outgrowth of a study that received a Boston Society of Architects (BSA) Research Grant in June 2004. The BSA jurors who reviewed the applications had four primary criteria in mind: likely contribution of the work proposed to the body of knowledge in the field of architecture; clarity of the proposed methodology; a clear plan for the dissemination of the results of the research; and the feasibility of the project as proposed. Doris Cole, F.A.I.A. and Jason, A.I.A. Knutson received the grant that helped to fund the study.

Cole and Goyette, Architects and Planners Inc. in Cambridge, Massachusetts provided additional funding and resources for both the study and the book.

A number of people contributed time and thoughts to this book. I wish to thank Jason Knutson, A.I.A., Harold Goyette, A.I.A., A.I.C.P., Theresa D'Amore, Eleena Zhelezov, Maria Natapov, and the many architects who patiently responded to inquiries. Special thanks go to Jason Knutson, A.I.A. who was my research partner in the study funded by the BSA Research Grant in 2004.

Mary Daniels, Librarian of Special Collections, Loeb Library at the Harvard Graduate School of Design provided helpful advise and guidance. Amy Vilelle of the International Archives of Women Architects at the Virginia Polytechnic Institute aided in the selection of images from the IAWA collection. The publisher, Cynthia Navaretta, of Midmarch Arts Press continued to be cheerfully encouraging and patient throughout the process.

The letters in this study have been edited to maintain confidentiality and anonymity of the respondents. The geographical locations of the letters have been indicated north, northwest, south, east, west, or midwest to enhance privacy. No parts of these letters are to be reproduced in any form or by any means, electronic, mechanical, photocopy, recording, or otherwise, without written permission. There is to be no breach of the confidentiality and anonymity of the respondents whether or not the author has been fully successful in the efforts to maintain the privacy of the respondents' letters.

The photographs have been generously provided by the various photographers, architects, organizations, and publications listed with each illustration. The photographs included in this book are only a sampling of the projects by women in architecture from 1946 to 2006 in the United States. Most of the illustrated projects are by respondents, but some others have been included which are relevant to this post World War II period. There were and are many more projects and architects to be considered and documented. Hopefully these few illustrations will encourage future research on projects by women in architecture.

Organization of Women Architects - San Francisco Bay Area (OWA) at
San Francisco Art Institute, April 15, 1973.
photo: courtesy, Jeremiah Bragstad Photographer.

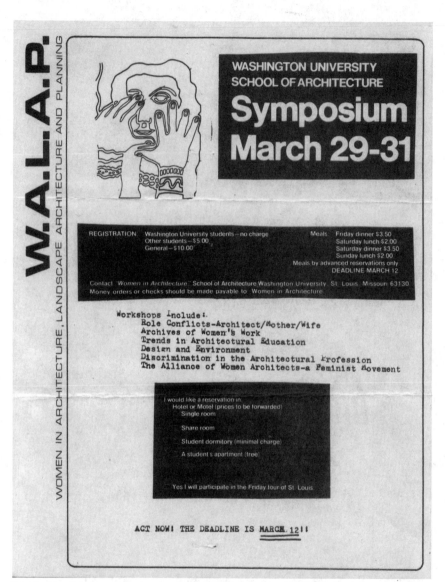

W.A.L.A.P., Women in Architecture, Landscape Architecture and Planning Newsletter, Boston, Massachusetts. Symposium at Washington University, St. Louis, Missouri, 1974.

INTRODUCTION

In the process of researching her first book on a history of women in architecture, *From Tipi to Skyscraper*, Doris Cole sent out an inquiry letter in 1972 to women architects throughout the country. The inquiry asked these women to provide comments and opinions on their training, professional development, goals, experiences with gender discrimination, and any other topics of personal and professional interest:

> Some of the questions I have in mind are as follows:
> What factors in life led you to architecture? Where
> did you receive your professional training? Have you
> practiced your profession? If you have not practiced,
> what were some of the reasons? What types of projects
> and what phases (design, working drawings, supervi-
> sion, etc.) of the projects have you done? Have you
> been subjected to discrimination in salary, job promo-
> tion, etc. due to your sex? What are some of your goals
> in architecture? Please don't feel limited to [these] few
> questions.[1]

Approximately sixty letters were received in reply, forty-three of which are transcribed, edited, and included in this book. These personal letters chronicle careers that spanned from the turn of the twentieth century through two World Wars, the Great Depression, and into the 1950s, 1960s, and 1970s. Another inquiry letter was sent out in 2004 so that more current views could be considered. Thirteen letters from 2004 and 2005 are included in this book. Also, two of the original respondents provided 2006 postscripts to bring us up to date on their careers.

RESEARCH METHOD

Women architects to whom the original 1970s inquiry was mailed were identified by consulting the membership rolls of national professional organizations and individual state boards of registration. These rolls tended to not identify individuals by sex, so educated guess work was used to identify women architects, with a few honest mistakes from time to time which resulted in some amusing responses[2] (and a few indignant ones, too). Hundreds of copies of the original inquiry were mailed to architects throughout the country.

The majority of respondents wrote back to Cole only once, taking the time to thoughtfully answer most of the questions and reflect on their careers in a single letter. Some, though, got more involved and wrote longer or multiple missives, sometimes straying a bit from the initial topics of interest: "I shall proceed rapidly, chatteringly, voluminously, to get an answer to you. This letter may end up being my autobiography."[3]

This current research reviewed a significant amount of material received in the 1970s, which included personal letters, resumes, press clippings, book passages, and marketing material. Of primary interest were the personal letters, where respondents expressed themselves outside the conventions of more business-like formats.

The letters themselves arrived in a variety of states. Some were carefully and formally presented on company letterhead, perhaps typed by the respondent's office staff. Others were hand-written, more casual and intimate. Already-legible letters were photocopied and edited for content and to make them generally anonymous. Hand-written letters were transcribed first and then edited in a similar fashion. In editing the letters for inclusion in this book, it was decided to try to retain the autobiographical candor of the women's responses while maintaining the privacy of the writers. Nearly all personal names, and most firm names, are obscured. The city and state locations of the respondents were replaced with more general geographical locations: north, northwest, south, east, west, mid west. The candid, personal nature of many of the letters provides a unique viewpoint into the observations and accomplishments of these women.

Multiplicity of voices is key. This monograph was prepared with no expectation of commonality. It is not the goal to define "women's roles" in architecture. There is no intention of reducing these or any women's experiences to fit a pre-determined story line. What is evident in the letters, though, are some common themes and shared viewpoints.

KEY FINDINGS

The letter writers told a variety of stories explaining the origins of their interests in architecture. Several had a family member in the profession of architecture or related fields like engineering who provided exposure, influence, and encouragement. Others exhibited interests or abilities as youngsters that were sometimes supported: "Daddy would remark, 'Wouldn't it be nice if our daughter would be an architect;'"[4] and sometimes discouraged: " . . . my teacher took me aside and in scolding me explained, the boys were supposed to build the house and the girls were to make the linens for it, and would I please go over with the girls and make a pillowcase."[5] A large number of writers commented that architecture was a combination of the artistic and the technical, and attributed their vocation to talents in both art and math: "I developed a great interest in art — and a small talent — and had no difficulty with math and that sort of thing;"[6] "I considered seriously what I might do with a talent for drawing and a mathematics major;"[7] "I wanted to study art and mathematics;"[8] " . . . it was the logical combination of my two favorite subjects — Art and Math;"[9] "As a girl I loved drawing — and mathematics — they seemed to point to architecture."[10]

The letter writers took a variety of paths in pursuit of their education as architects. During the early part of the twentieth century, it was not uncommon for women from around the country to attend some of the more established East Coast universities such as Columbia, M.I.T., and Cornell. Land grant universities, founded throughout the country starting in the mid-nineteenth century, were also among the first to admit women to professional degree programs, largely because they were required to do so by law. As populations shifted, more and more state and private universities expanded their architecture programs. By the 1930s, 1940s, and 1950s, more women reported earning degrees at schools of architecture in the West and Midwest as well. To many women, a degree in architecture was often seen as a way to gain practical skills with which to earn a living: "A liberal arts education is a beautiful thing, but what does one do with it? . . . I crossed Broadway to Avery Hall and was encouraged . . . to enter the School of Architecture."[11]

For the most part, these women found themselves welcome at most schools and universities, and reported little out-right discrimination in their education: "Both Columbia and M.I.T. were entirely without prejudice as far as women were concerned."[12] Female students of architecture did stand out as uncommon in their classes and studios, and more often found themselves to be the recipients of good-natured teasing than scornful reproach. While some women avoided attention: "I kept to myself and tried to be inconspicuous,"[13] others competed for and attained academic recognition: "In fact, I left Columbia with all the academic honors . . . and then picked up more at M.I.T."[14]

World War II brought with it many new opportunities for women to learn and apply professional skills. Many future archi-tects received their first training in fields related to architecture as a direct result of participating in the war effort: "Although majoring in chemistry in college, I took intensive engineering and drafting during the Second World War."[15] Those with de-grees already in hand also found employment - by choice or ne-cessity — in the military or in war-related manufacturing firms: "World War II was in progress so I went to work for 'Uncle Sam' first with the Army Engineers then transferred to the Air Force where I taught map drafting and plotted air fields all over the world."[16] These experiences exposed women architects to greater professional responsibility and encouraged them to pursue their education and careers in earnest after the war ended.

No factor appeared to affect women's participation in the profession of architecture as much as marriage and raising a family. It was not uncommon for some of the respondents to give up their formal careers in architecture altogether upon getting married or having children: "At the end of five years I married and devoted the next ten or more years to raising a family . . . I never went back to an architect's office."[17] Almost all mar-ried women architects who responded to the 1970s inquiry had to balance their commitments to family with their aspirations in architecture. Often, it was necessary for women to remove themselves from the practice of architecture for some time. "I can divide my life into three parts — 25 years to grow up physi-cally, 20 years with the mother major, and now 20 to 40 years as a professional architect,"[18] which led to delays in professional advancement and difficulties competing with men who did not bear the same familial responsibilities. Some women architects often found it necessary to make choices between career and family: "I find running a household is an obligation and cannot let my professional ambitions overwhelm my private life."[19]

Many women architects custom tailored their practice of architecture to fit their own life choices. Some grew successful private practices out of their own home: "After a few years, I had a full-time housekeeper, a part-time secretary, and two part-time draftsmen. At this point my husband insisted that I move the business into an office. . . ."[20] Others started partnerships with architect husbands, where some aspects of both domestic and business responsibilities could be shared with more flexibility. Several writers acknowledged the importance of support and encouragement from their spouses: "You can see that having a husband who was sympathetic to the problems of women has been of great importance to me in trying to be a career woman."[21]

The letters received in the 1970s showcased a remarkable variety of professional experiences. Many women owned their own businesses, from part-time sole proprietorships to large corporate firms. Women were represented in all manner of roles in traditional architecture firms, including draftsperson, designer, project manager, and department head. It is especially interesting (perhaps exposing one of our own pre-conceptions) to note the number of women who reported that they specialized in construction documents production. These women architects designed houses, schools, churches, factories, offices, apartment buildings — nearly every building type. Some women were developing innovations in building technology such as tilt-wall construction and heat-recovery systems, and still others pursued alternative career paths such as residential design-build and campus planning.

While women architects were represented in nearly all roles and job types, experience with discrimination is discussed in nearly all of the letters. Yet, interestingly, there are few consistent or pervasive trends. Women's perceptions of discrimination were personal and often unique. Examples of discrimination were reported at the level of the "institutions" of architecture such as universities: ". . . . we don't want you but since the school is co-educational and state owned we have to take you if you insist;"[22] professional organizations: "Are the boys at the AIA meetings really unfriendly, or are they just afraid they might have to buy me a drink?"[23] and large firms: "I was told, for example, when asking for an interview at Skidmore's New York office, 'we don't hire women'. I was so taken aback that I blurted 'oh, I thought yours was a firm of *modern* architects.'"[24] More common was discrimination on a day-to-day level. Women complained of limitation in opportunities for responsibility and advancement in architecture firms. Pay rates were commonly reported to be lower than those of male colleagues, the excuse usually being that women "didn't have a family to support."[25]

In their practices, women architects often had to confront an old pre-conception that they were best suited for design of domestic architecture: " . . . I have found that opportunities for high rise buildings have been scarce due to sex discrimination; however, individual large custom homes (emphasis on kitchens) have been more than plentiful and lucrative due to the fact that I am a woman."[26]

Interestingly, some women architects recognized this bias and used it to the best of their advantage: "On the other hand, once into the profession women architects do have some bonuses. There is a general notion that they are bound to be good in residential work. . . ."[27] One architect's comment seems to both propagate and capitalize on prevailing assumptions about women's expertise in design for the home:

> I plan to remain in residential Architecture with my
> own practice because I do think a woman has an ad-
> vantage in this area, particularly if she has had expe-
> rience in keeping house & raising a family. She should
> have a little better insight concerning how a house
> should work — it's an ideal situation for a woman.[28]

It was frequently taken for granted that women architects were endowed with artistic sensibilities but lacked technical abilities. Even an early advocate of women's education and involvement in architecture, Henry Frost, reverted to widely held cultural stereotypes when he suggested that architecture appealed to "the naturally artistic feminine instinct," that "the woman student has a tendency towards the more delicate side of design, the more intimate scheme," and that women were "likely to have a better sense of color and detail."[29] As already stated, such popular preconceptions clearly affected women's roles in the profession (e.g. — design of single family residences versus supervision of high rise construction). One woman was amused to report: " . . . when it comes to color and finish selection, my being a woman has the men bamboozled. After all everyone knows that girls know all about color. I am completely ignorant about color."[30]

Another preconceived notion encountered by many women architects was that they were not suited to participate in onsite construction supervision activities. As male-dominated as the architecture profession is, the building industry is even more so. Women found themselves excluded from the job site due to tradition: "Women are rarely allowed to supervise construction here due, I'm told, to superstitions in the construction trade;"[31] resentment: " . . . the building trades are impossible — I've been told too often to go back to the kitchen where I belong;"[32] and an impulse to protect "the fairer sex": "Most of my employers/clients alike have reservations about a woman with contractors. They are afraid that I would either pick up the rough language or swoon instead. It is difficult to play the happy medium."[33] One architect devised her own successful strategy for gaining acceptance on the job site: "While it is sometimes ticklish, I have learned that the wisest course is to protect the workmen's ego and it works well. It is as though they want to show off their work for me to receive the praise which I lavish. So you can call it a kind of corruption on my part."[34]

As varied as these women architect's experiences were, so too were their stated goals. Some women voiced rather pragmatic objectives, to continue building a successful career or business: "My goals are very mundane at this point. The first priority is to restructure our practice into a diversified firm . . ."[35] "As for my goals in architecture, I am contented to be a job captain and deliver a competent set of working drawings."[36] Several women thought of their career as a means to explore and support broader interests in the world: "My goals are to . . . study people, places, and the endless possibilities in this world."[37] A number of letter writers recognized the possibilities of architecture to improve the world and expressed a desire to contribute to that process: "My goals are simply to reflect the individuality and needs of people to the best of my ability, and to design so that the structure will be in harmony."[38] One woman succinctly expressed her desire to make a difference in the world by trying "to help solve some of the many social problems, and to work towards better planning and design."[39]

CONCLUSION

This book serves as a resource, a collection of personal, candid reflections. Few previous studies have incorporated the first-hand accounts of women's real-world experiences and feelings. The writers of the letters in this volume represent a broad cross-section of professional women of various ages, experience levels, and accomplishments. Some letters describe the struggles of young women competing for opportunities and advancement, while others come from women secure in their achievements. The letters chronicle over fifty years of the history of the United States, and document the impact of wars, depressions, and evolving social, political, and cultural norms on women's pursuits in architecture. Indeed, the value of this collection is the multiplicity of experiences described.

The letters are a testimony to the grit, humor, pathos, and determination of these women architects, whose goal was to be full participants in constructing a better world. Through laughter and tears, success and frustration, these women pushed on. Their stories can be an inspiration to all architects, of all backgrounds, who may be facing similar challenges today.

New contemporary observations were also obtained from current women architects as well. In the autumn of 2004, another inquiry letter, along with the original 1972 letter, was prepared and sent to hundreds of practitioners across the U.S. The same open-ended questions were asked. The goal was to learn what differences had occurred over the course of thirty years. During these thirty years there had been the introduction of affirmative action policies which made a real difference in terms of women's access to the professions. In spite of women's increasing participation, leadership, and success in the practice of architecture, it was surprising to find that not much had changed. These new letters contained stories of successes and failures, challenges and choices, frustrations and achievements very similar to those from the 1970s.

The importance of women's contributions to and participation in architecture is becoming more recognized. The quantity, strength, and influence of organizations supporting women's roles in architecture continue to increase, and the profession is beginning to acknowledge the benefits of diversity in the practice of architecture. It is hoped that more women's voices can be added to make the production of the built environment truly representative of the values and aspirations of our entire culture.

NOTES

1. See Appendices, Original Inquiry Letter, 1972
2. Letter No. 1, page 1
3. Letter No. 4, page 1
4. Letter No. 11, page 1
5. Letter No. 5, page 2
6. Letter No. 11, page 1
7. Letter No. 12, page 1
8. Letter No. 32, page 1
9. Letter No. 38, page 1
10. Letter No. 39, page 1
11. Letter No. 4, page 1
12. Letter No. 12, page 1
13. Letter No. 23, page 2
14. Letter No. 12, page 1
15. Letter No. 16, page 1
16. Letter No. 34, page 2
17. Letter No. 28, page 1
18. Letter No. 4, page 7
19. Letter No. 3, page 2
20. Letter No. 15, page 3
21. Letter No. 6, page 3
22. Letter No. 32, page1
23. Letter No. 4, page 5
24. Letter No. 12, page 1
25. Letter No. 11, page 2
26. Letter No. 16, page 1
27. Letter No. 17, page 3
28. Letter No. 38, page 2
29. Doris Cole, *From Tipi to Skyscraper: A History of Women in Architecture*, (Cambridge i Press, 1973) 80–81.
30. Letter No. 4, page 5
31. Letter No. 7, page 2
32. Letter No. 38, page 2
33. Letter No. 3, page 1
34. Letter No. 6, page 5
35. Letter No. 21, page 1
36. Letter No. 43, page 2
37. Letter No. 4, page 7
38. Letter No. 10, page 2
39. Letter No. 9, page 1

Eleanor Raymond with Maria Telkes: Solar Heated House, Dover, Massachusetts, 1948. photo: courtesy, D. Cole.

Eleanor Raymond: Warner House, Ipswich, Massachusetts, 1951.
photo: courtesy, D. Cole.

Eleanor Raymond: Nichols Factory Addition, Waltham, Massachusetts, 1959.
photo: courtesy, Hutchins Photography Inc.

Lucille Raport: Mountain Retreat, Arrowhead Lake, California, 1948.
photo: courtesy, Southwest Builder and Contractor, 1960.

Lucille Raport: Oakwood School, Moorpark, California. photo: courtesy, Southwest Builder and Contractor, 1960.

Lucille Raport: Canby-East Apartments, Los Angeles, California. photo: courtesy, Southwest Builder and Contractor, 1960.

LETTER NO. 1
December 1, 1972
West

There really was no way I could answer your inquiry which would have been relevant. You see I am blessed with the first name 'Beverley' which is the male spelling of the old English name. Since the majority of the populace do not know the woman's spelling is 'Beverly' I have dropped the first name professionally. Perhaps this gives credence to the discrimination theory because I did drop the name to eliminate confusion.

I do honestly believe that in the art fields that there is very little discrimination, however, that fact is muted by the mere deletion of the female first name. As you can imagine from about the age of eight years I have had some interesting experiences with this first name. Two of them: being placed upon WAC shipping orders during WW II and continually being 'rushed' by the sororities while attending the University of California. And then there is 'Avon', 'Spencer Corsets', 'Maiden Form. . . .

LETTER NO. 2
1972
West

Beginning. My parents were sharp in math, and Mother an artist, too.

We built "club houses" when we were little, including the plans for an adobe one (a square paper sheet with each layer of bricks figured out and pinned together in a tablet)) but we ran out of steam before we had enough bricks made. I didn't remember making all the details on paper; but it turned up when Mom and Dad retired and sorted everything out! Also, I enjoyed sewing . . . inventing patterns for my dolls, and especially for my little sister. Let's call it "three dimension" understanding. My sister, ten years younger, was a math major in college for two years and then switched to Architecture as she wasn't interested in a teaching career. She hasn't done much with it . . . family still at home, and in the L.A. area, mostly remodeling jobs turn up. . . .

We both graduated from U.C., Berkeley; I in 1939 and she was probably 1950. My class started with 80 members, and three girls included. About one third finished in the class . . . but all three girls did!! In my sister's class there were about 17 girls . . . but I'm sure they didn't all finish . . . same as the boys didn't all finish.

I married right out of school . . . and very gradually got my experience doing occasional plans for friends, etc. . . . I didn't work in an office at all . . . so neither got the training there, nor the "possible discrimination." However, one well-meaning person told me never learn to type, or that would be my job if I did work in a large office.

Moving to this area . . . was the turning point for me. My children were older . . . and building was booming. I had been doing work for one contractor for about 8 years previous to this move . . . and really got my practical training from him . . . on how to simplify framing, etc. . . . to hold costs and not lose effect or space. In my business everything is referral . . . so gradually over the years . . . the referrals have snowballed . . . and I have many more private clients than contractors . . . also, building conditions have changed, where once, contractors could build anything . . . and it sold; now there is less demand . . . and more small contractors are bidding on jobs rather than speculative building themselves. If there is any discrimination . . . it would occur before I am contacted, and I wouldn't be aware of it; most people who do come to me are delighted to have a woman planning the interior of a home . . . and usually no problems with the exterior, either. I complete working drawings and a list of general specifications, and the client takes over on selecting a contractor, and generally knows the house well enough to spot any error in framing, for instance . . . so with the county or city plan check and inspections on the job . . . I am not needed, nor do I have to charge for the extra time. Last year I completed plans for thirty houses and about 20 additions; everyone delighted with their plans. This is a great field . . . since people are so delighted to be building and happy with the end product . . . I really recommend it!!

Often, I have been asked, "Doesn't it really thrill me to see my finished building?" And of course it does; but I find that when my clients are thrilled because we have achieved their "dream come true"; and they are so happy in their new home . . . this is to me the best possible thank you. I have no goal for building "monuments" for my sake; but the right house for each client; a very satisfying goal for me.

On the math situation, a few more comments in general. . . . Mom taught 6th grade with her college certificate (no teacher training in those days) and the previous teachers had neglected the math (probably weak in it), so Mom got her class through 3rd to 7th grade in Math and had no problems with it. (Women and Math comment.) Math was my easiest subject in High School. . . . My daughter went into Sociology, though her High School Science teachers thought she should stay with science. In Sociology, as in Nursing . . . Math ability is rare . . . and she understands all the analyzing and graph studies . . . runs the computer for her results of surveys . . . so the Math background is the key in these areas, too.

P.S. I forgot to mention that my office is in my home — and I have no employees — so I'm the secretary, draftsman, etc., but also my time is my own (*if* I weren't so busy!).

P.S.S. November 3, 2006

To add to my original letter, I worked successfully until I was 80 and then retired. (I'm now almost 89). I had almost 200 projects in the 50 years — mainly in Contra Costa County. Several of them were large construction companies and some small ones and many individuals. It was so great to have such appreciative clients as I designed their dream homes.

My sister, in Culver City near Los Angeles, is also an Architect and has been busy for many years — all referrals, like mine and she is 78 and still busy working. Her eldest daughter, studied Italian and Oceanography in college and then dropped out. She got interested in architecture and went to work for an architectural firm in Santa Cruz. After 10 years experience, she studied for the Architecture License exam and passed. Now she is working at home, too, with enough referrals to do well.

LETTER NO. 3
May 16, 1972
West

I was in Hong Kong when entering college. Selection of majors was limited. "Architecture" was selected by a process of elimination! I spent three years at University of Hong Kong under the R.I.B.A. system from 1953–56, then one year at University of Oregon, Eugene, Oregon, then two years at University of California, Berkeley, California and received Bachelor of Architecture 1959. My current interest is to be able to work on new towns in the near future. . . .

First of all by the time anyone becomes an "architect," one has gone through training, examinations, and working with others in the same profession. The license puts us in a recognized standing such as lawyers, doctors, engineers. . . . I have not had any insurmountable obstacle (yet) in professional advancement although I do wonder if things couldn't be easier otherwise. Such standards are tangible and can happen to anyone, man or woman. Being a woman, any advantage is very much offset by the disadvantage. Male colleagues, clients, etc. alike regard me with caution almost always at first. Later on, given the opportunity to work together, they are, most of the time, easy to work with. As a matter of fact, I am so used to working with men, I find working with women more difficult.

Most of my employers/clients alike, have reservations about a woman with contractors. They are afraid that I would either pick up the rough language or swoon instead. It is difficult to play the happy medium.

I have not started a private practice although most of my friends have. Having your own office seems to be the goal of architects of my vintage. I find running a household is an obligation and cannot let my professional ambitions overwhelm my private life. I have not had the feeling of quitting altogether (i.e. my profession) although I have changed jobs from time to time when there is lack of challenge. To simply stay at home would drive me out of my mind (I think). I had a taste of it when taking six weeks for the first child and three weeks for the second. I have worked, since graduating from college in 1959, for three different architects, one manufacturing company, and University of California at Santa Cruz Physical Planning and Construction.

LETTER NO. 4
May 12, 1972
West

I shall proceed rapidly, chatteringly, voluminously, to get an answer to you. This letter may end up being my autobiography.

The factors which led to my choice of architecture were not of the Road to Damascus variety. I was studying at Barnard College at the time, the most expensive school in the U.S. I had been told by being valedictorian in high school that I was very smart. I needed however, to be graduated from a school of higher learning with some kind of a trade, in order to be able to earn a living. A liberal arts education is a beautiful thing, but what does one do with it? Teach? Go on to more graduate work and expense for Papa? I crossed Broadway to Avery Hall and was encouraged by Dean Arnaud to enter the School of Architecture. There were not very many freshmen in Sept. 1945, most of the men still being in the War. Our freshman class had 6 men and 6 women. Of the women, 3, I believe were finally graduated, while the number of men increased. I wonder if I would have been accepted if there had not been a lack of scholars at the time. I must point out that I was not gloriously filled with the wonders of architecture, just was good in Art and as I said, very smart. Surprisingly, they never threw me out, for I really was not too clever, but they even graduated me in 1950. It was a four-year course but I had taken a year off to earn some money. I was graduated in June 10, 1950, and on June 18, 1950, my first child was born. Terrible planning, but in those days, one just did not get an abortion.

I had my last child in 1955. Around 1960, ten years of convent life, I went to work in order to gain 8 months of office experience to be admitted to the State Licensing Exams. My husband, was at the time a licensed civil engineer in partnership with an architect. I was finally licensed in 1962 plus or minus.

After my last child was in first grade, I began going to the office full-time. And did the whole career, mommy, wife, cook, and housekeeper bit. I had very little help in the major housework, enlisting by force the children too. Do you know how many hours a woman spends in the grocery store in a year?

During these years I was the chief designer at the office, because there was no one else to do that work. Good men designers are not only hard to find but they also have a tendency to open their own offices if they have anything on the ball. We worked on a large office building for the Juvenile Dept., a branch library, but mostly schools. I also did the colored renderings for presentation, professional renderers being very expensive.

The firm eventually became the great husband-wife team. All this time, I had found working with my husband a very trying situation.

Can you imagine seeing someone 24 hours a day? You eat breakfast together, work together, lunch together, have dinner together, and then sleep together. It becomes an incestuous situation. Then you go to the beach together, the movies, church. Ugh! If you can survive that, you can live through all sorts of rigors.

This mama-papa candy-store operation drove me wild. We could not even take a decent vacation. So we went looking for a partner, one who would not eat us up alive, one who did not believe he was the world's greatest designer, one who could work with a woman-Partner. That last was an eye-opener for me. All those fine courteous gentlemen who are afraid of women. But I am being kind in thinking they just have no balls. Finally we merged but I am not a full partner now. There are many aspects of the work which bore me. When I work for the firm I am paid on the hourly basis. I hate keeping a time sheet, but I like being paid. All those years with my husband I received no salary. I also resumed my maiden name for the purposes of the letterhead, . . . I still sign documents with my legal name, and have had a little trouble with the Board on use of a fictitious name. But I think they are afraid I might get Women's Lib after them if they make too much noise. Dean Arnaud had told me to keep my maiden name, just as Miss Frances Perkins did. I did not heed his good advice because my young and immature husband did not like to be called by my name. And being a product of that time, I succumbed as all good sweet girls would. Especially the stupid ones.

The part of the work that I love concerns site planning, major layout, planning, trying to interpret the not-too-well expressed desires and needs of the client; I am tireless and dauntless with overlay over overlay to achieve the best solution. I have a simple belief that if it is there on the paper and if anyone can find it, I can; I never see any design as a stock solution. In a small office such as ours, we are all working on everything. I do the preliminary drawings, interpret the client conference meetings, oversee the working drawings, decide many of the specification items, and go to the job for the supervision. My partners do much of the supervision. I don't do any of these things alone. We have a wonderful exchange of ideas, full-tongued disagreements, and a fearless openness about discussion and brain-storming. It is difficult to achieve this openness in a group, no fear of treading on delicate little toes and egos. Respect and love for one another. I used to be afraid of hurting any male ego. Afraid of criticizing the work of some nitwit draftsman.

In my long-winded story of my career, you can see that I have been protected (aided and abetted, too) by my husband. Lately, there not being much work at the office I have been staying home and have done some thinking. I read Germaine Greer's book and feel enlightened by many of her ideas on the subject of male and female eunuchs. My major feeling now, at this moment, is that the discrimination was in Myself. Something has been wrong for years, and much of it has been a lack of faith in my own capabilities. Perhaps it is caused by the little needles from the men that I allow to bother me, perhaps I feel that girls just are not as smart as men, perhaps I really am no talented architect. I do not mean to deny that women have been discriminated in the field; it is just that I have not felt it overwhelmingly, except in myself.

Are the boys at the A.I.A. meetings really unfriendly, or are they just afraid they might have to buy me a drink? Women's Lib got to them last year and they wanted me on the Board. Their token female. Why did that nitwit say, "you must be a good cook"? What does that have to do with a design conference on a school kitchen? But he was a near imbecile anyway.

I am at the point now where I think these men are to be pitied, that the fault is in myself if I allow their remarks to bother me. Great what ego will do for you. Just now in looking for clients, my husband pushes the fact that one of the partners is a female. Even Ma Bell may kowtow to that one. Public opinion is getting to the telephone company.

On the other hand, I must say, that when it comes to color and finish selection, my being a woman has the men bamboozled. After all everyone knows that girls know all about color. I am completely ignorant about color. I have not as yet seen a real study on color, as it affects people. But I hit little opposition in my color work. Also people ask if I "do" houses. Sure I'll do houses if there is any money in it. I'd love to do some low-cost and some high class. Every architect would say the same.

There has been a dearth of work lately, not only at our office but also in general in the Bay Area, due to the depression, I suppose. My husband has been doing a lot of belly-aching about it all. I have generally left the job-hunting up to him. We never got a commission from an interview at which I was present. Our jobs have come over the phone. I tried Soroptimists for awhile, just for business contacts, but found no hope among secretaries. The only extra-curricular do-good organization I have been at all interested in has been the Friends of the Library. Now I am out of that too, for a year at least. Someday, women will be admitted to Rotary.

I was leading up to something in that last paragraph but got side-tracked. We haven't been very successful in getting work lately. Our partner is not an aggressive person, my husband hates cold-turkey calls (feels it is demeaning, somehow), and I have been the pure artiste. I have been reading a very interesting book, purchased and touted by my husband, Marketing Architectural and Engineering Services by Weld Coxe, (Van Nostrand Reinhold and Co.) He, the author, has given us a new lease on life, and we are preparing to go plan a new campaign on selling our services. I am quite fascinated by the whole procedure, and also feel that a few years ago when I was young and beautiful and sexy, I could not have approached this matter with the cold calculation that I feel today.

Now, at the advanced age of 46, I feel I am ready to begin. Not begin again, just begin. I can divide my life into three parts — 25 years to grow up physically, 20 years with the mother major, and now 20 to 40 years as a professional architect. The work I have done up to now had been in the manner of an apprentice. Fortunately, I kept my "hand in," but now that my children can be more independent of me, I can forge ahead. Just selfishly do what I want to do.

My goals are to get work, so we can eat and pay tuition, and to study people, places, and the endless possibilities in this world. What do people really enjoy? Why are some spaces unpleasant, some heart-warming? I want to travel and really read Ada Louis Huxtable. I want to design parks, playgrounds even maybe churches, without that silly symbolism. I want to write articles, when I have learned something. The study of architecture is endless, and you do not have to be a young chit to do a humane job. Tomorrow, I shall think of more to say, but that's enough for now.

LETTER NO. 5
May 15, 1972
South

I am a practicing architect. I have been with this firm since graduation. I became an associate in 1965 and a full partner the first of this year. Our firm produces structural engineering and master planning as well as performing architectural services. We do buildings of all types: medical, educational, religious, recreational, financial, offices, commercial, industrial and military come to mind quickly. We have done work throughout Texas and to a lesser degree in Oklahoma, New Mexico, and Arkansas.

I cannot say why I became an architect. No one in my very large family has ever been engaged in a building trade to my knowledge. I feel as though I simply have always followed the course of least resistance and this is where it led me.

I can clearly remember the first time I encountered the word "architect." It was in my first grade reader. The teacher patiently explained to the class "an architect plans houses, decides where the windows and doors are to be and things like that." We must have shown interest, because she started hurrying each class slightly to gain an extra twenty minutes at the end of each day to erect a wood frame house and cover it with a skin of cardboard. My recollection of that experience is one of frustration.

I never seemed to do much — just be in someone else's way. One day my teacher took me aside and in scolding me explained, the boys were supposed to build the house and the girls were to make the linens for it, and would I please go over with the girls and make a pillowcase. I did, and as I sewed, I realized for the first time that girls had one type duty and the boys another in this world of ours. I also realized that the boys were having a whole lot more fun building the house than I was having making that pillowcase.

I enrolled in Architecture at Texas Technological College (now Texas Tech University) in 1950. Taking some bad advice, I chose the design option. I would have chosen the construction option if I had known what I know now.

Taking some good advice, "if a woman is going to perform a man's task, she must be more capable than a man doing the same task," I gave it all I had and have continued to do so ever since.

My father passed away at the end of my second year in Architecture and in order to pay my expenses, I took a job working for the Landscaping Department at Tech and for the City Parks and Recreational Department. This gave me valuable drafting and design experience, and also some pretty valuable *money*.

I received the local A.I.A. Chapter Award as the outstanding graduating student in Architecture in 1955.

Of course, I have met my share of discrimination. Overcoming it helps make the outcome more pleasant. I feel that it has taken me twice as long to progress in this profession as it would have taken if I were not female. I have had wonderful encouragement from some of the finest men anyone could hope to know.

I am not much for women's lib. I believe a woman must prove herself qualified if she undertakes a job normally done by a male. If she does this, she should insist on being paid and respected for her capabilities and accomplishments. She must always remember that she is first of all a lady.

LETTER NO. 6
May 11, 1972
West

Germaine Greer refers briefly but significantly to women in architecture in her book *The Female Eunuch*. Her statement, as I recall points out that among all the major professions women architects constitute the tiniest percentage of the total architects — something less than one percent. I don't know how accurate her statistics are, I think she was quoting the Bureau of Labor Statistics.

I wrote a letter to the national office of the AIA a couple years ago asking about the number of women architects in the U.S. and they answered that their organization lists only 195. This does not fully answer the question, of course, because of the number who are either not members of the AIA or for many reasons we both know, have retired from the profession. My own count of the number in California (from the roster of registered architects) is about 75 — unless there are a few named Joseph or Bill and some men who are named Jean or Elizabeth. . . . California has about 7000 registered architects.

So, as a friend of mine remarked when I gave the statistics, "You're not rare, you're a freak. You're not even a minority, you're a minusculity." There just may be more one-eyed male architects than women.

The emphasis on education was overwhelming in our family of Russian-Jewish immigrants. These hardy people, to whom education was denied, put COLLEGE at the top of their list of aspirations for their luckier American born children. I never felt that I was being educated (at great hardship to themselves) in order to prepare myself for a "good" marriage. I was supposed to be Something — a scientist, a professor, a musician — a somebody with a title.

Actually, when I came home one day from high school and announced that I had decided to be an Architect they took the news gravely and respectfully. But I think they were as astonished as if I had said I wanted to be a professional boxer and that if I pursued this unlikely goal I would start to grow hair on my chest. My sister was already in pre-med and they were both delighted and unmystified by her choice. . . .

I took three years of architecture at Univ. of Calif., Berkeley and the final two years at USC. I graduated in 1947. I am 53. I got my license in 1956. Meanwhile I had three children. One died soon after birth. The other two are girls. One is 24, a graduate from Univ. Of Calif. at Santa Barbara, the other is 22 and a student at Santa Cruz. My elder daughter is pursuing a career in Journalism, is somewhat radical politically and is active in Women's Lib. My younger daughter is a very fine artist, very serious about her work and somewhat a hippie.

My husband is a screenwriter of some note. He wrote the screenplays of "Bridge on the River Kwai," "Lawrence of Arabia," "Place in the Sun" (he got an Oscar for that one), "Friendly Persuasion," "Planet of the Apes" (the first one), and other less notable.

After graduation I worked a year and a half for the Los Angeles Planning Dept. Then I became pregnant and was out of commission for about a year.

I worked while in school for Raymond Schindler for no money and later for very little money for various small offices. I took time out to have another child and then went to work for Daniel, Mann, Johnson and Mendenhall. They gave me the honor of being chief color consultant, a job not unusually reserved for women architects. However, I was able to get out on the jobs during construction for the finishing work, which was a good experience and better than the other junior draftsmen were getting. I was fired after two years because of an article about my husband which appeared in Time magazine. He was by then a blacklisted writer and had written a film called "Salt of the Earth" which at that time was considered subversive. It was, in fact, very mild when viewed in today's context. The subject was taken from life. It was about a strike in the Silver mines of New Mexico, involving many Mexican Americans. There was an injunction prohibiting the men from picketing and so their wives took over and won the strike for the men. It was one of the first of the films on the role of women in society and how they developed in a crisis situation. You can see that having a husband who was sympathetic to the problems of women has been of great importance to me in trying to be a career woman. He has been a tremendous help to me in encouragement and sympathy when the going was rough.

I worked for a couple years for Richard Neutra, a couple for Victor Gruen and Assoc. In both of these offices I functioned as a senior draftsman. The jobs were large ones — high rise office buildings, a university, banks, schools, etc. I did no supervision. Other draftsmen doing comparable work were getting higher salaries than I. I have always been subject to a certain amount of sexist attitudes on many counts — reluctance to give full responsibility, sexual overtures, both subtle and overt, lower pay, etc. When I had finally achieved the position of job captain there were men who refused to work on my team. It happened seldom but often enough to be upsetting.

I was once refused a job because there was no ladies room. But, in general, I did manage to find work easily in the late 1940s and 50s. I have been in two partnerships. Both were failures. From 1956 through 1964 I lived in France. My husband found it easier to work there during the McCarthy period. I took some courses in Urbanism at the Ecole de Beaux Arts. Also I sculpted (a secret ambition for a long time) and traveled. I worked in the office of a French Architect for about 6 months — which is a story in itself, too long to tell here. I am a member of the L'Union Internationale de Femmes Architectes. I have never been to one of their yearly meetings which are held in very exotic places but I do intend to go someday. I get lots of correspondence from them all hilariously translated into English.

In 1967 I finally opened my own office. The town we live in is quite small, but only one hour from L.A. It's been a terrible struggle to get my office on its feet, and frankly, I don't know if it's a case of discrimination or simply that it's hard to get a new office going. Probably both. I've had some lean years and some less lean. In 1970 my office started to expand its operations and now I have two draftsmen and am interested in taking on a partner. My jobs have been small ones — residences, small businesses, churches, apts. Oddly enough, I have had quite a bit of publicity (more than most architects in similar situations) precisely because of being a woman architect running her own office. There have been two or three articles about me in local and county newspapers and I had a house published in the home section in color in the Los Angeles Times. Supervision has turned out to be less difficult as a woman than I had anticipated. While it is sometimes ticklish, I have learned that the wisest course is to protect the workmen's ego and it works well. It is as though they want to show off their work for me to receive the praise which I lavish. So you can call it a kind of corruption on my part. But I like to believe that we all need appreciation and if they have not been getting it from other male architects then I have a secret for success which has nothing to do with my gender.

LETTER NO. 7
May 10, 1972
East

My background is in art and architecture. I have a Bachelor of Fine Arts degree in Sculpture from the University of Nebraska, a Certificate of Architecture from The Cooper Union in New York City and a Bachelor of Arts degree in Architecture from Carnegie Institute of Technology (now Carnegie-Mellon University). I have worked in the field in Nebraska, New York and Pennsylvania. I am registered to practice in the states of Pennsylvania and Texas and am certified with the NCARB. Since 1950 I have been employed by eighteen different architectural firms and one contracting firm and am presently in the process of trying to build enough business to begin private practice.

I am the daughter of a Civil Engineer, so my exposure to construction came at a very early age and probably had a good deal of influence on my choice of architecture as a profession. I have practiced the profession under my own name on a limited basis, mostly residential and small alteration type work, but my experience under the name of others has been most varied. Most recently my involvement has been with high-rise and townhouse type HUD-FHA sponsored housing projects, but I have also been project architect for building types industrial, commercial and institutional.

During the six years I worked in New York City I found very little discrimination due to sex. Pittsburgh, however, is a different matter. Pittsburgh is a very provincial town, sometimes I think almost to the point of being backward. Salary and promotional advancements are obtained here by both sexes mainly by changing jobs. The contention here is that women, particularly single women, need less to live on than men, therefore they are paid less and since they don't tend to change jobs as easily or quickly as men their salary advancement is slow. Women are rarely allowed to supervise construction here due I'm told to superstitions in the construction trade. Last year for example Turner Construction Company issued an invitation to the local

Chapter of the AIA to inspect the construction of the U.S. Steel building. Several women accepted the invitation. Turner Construction replied that it could not allow women on the job site. I will not give note of the telephone calls I made, suffice to say we were allowed to attend the inspection. I have noted an encouraging change over the ten years I've been in Pittsburgh toward a more open attitude and feel with time that the city's provinciality will be overcome.

I have had many discouragements over the past 22 years but I believe, given the choice again, I would again choose architecture. The rewards greatly outweigh the disappointments.

LETTER NO. 8
April 29, 1972
Northwest

I have had a romance going with architecture for quite a few years now. I really love this field although at times it scares me.

You might say I was led into the architectural field by a mother who was always designing and building something, and by the results of a high school interest test I took, which indicated either a business or architectural field.

Being female, I was urged into the business field. That was a mistake and after a brief absence from school, I entered WSU in Architectural Engineering, graduating in 1946.

I looked for a job in the larger offices in Portland, Ore. to no avail and to my own good fortune which I was to realize later. I did find a job with Day Hilborn (now deceased) in Vancouver, Wash. He was an excellent teacher in all fields and gave a person as much responsibility as they were willing to take.

After working for him for 4 years, I accepted a position in a large Portland firm which I found stagnating. I stayed there 1 1/2 years and moved on to another small office. This was the only place I found any real prejudice and low pay from the principal.

Needless to say I moved on, this time to a medium-sized firm, where I enjoyed working very much.

In the meantime, I had married and my husband encouraged me to take my exam. I received my license in 1957, coinciding with the birth of our second of four children.

At this point it was impossible to work full time but since that time I worked in various offices by the job. Really much more interesting and this has kept me up with new materials and developments. I also did some on my own but felt this too difficult to continue responsibility wise, while my children were small.

Last fall with the death of one of the men I had occasionally worked with, I joined his associate to finish out the work in the office. We have joined forces with another architect in Vancouver on other jobs pending. (The Associate is also a woman going for her license in Washington this year.)

At the moment we are snowed under with low cost housing projects. We finished a credit union bank just before Christmas and a bowling alley last month.

Over the years I have worked on many various projects such as: residences, churches, schools, factory remodeling, housing for the aged, a mausoleum, store remodeling, mobile home (luxury) layouts, and others.

Of discrimination — it goes both ways. Being a woman in this field was a novelty and the established firms were generally able and willing to push you along as fast as you were willing to go. With the men doing the same work as I was, it was a matter of proving yourself and being tactful.

At present I find women are pretty well accepted, but they and the young men coming out of school these days are all having a difficult time finding jobs in firms willing to give them adequate training.

As to goals, only time can tell, I know I will stay in the field and perhaps after my children are on their own open an office of my own, hoping to be busy enough to hire some of these young people and do what was done for me.

Barbara Durand, partner at Durand Designs, Inc.: Private Residence, Fullerton, California, 1961.
photo: courtesy, John Upton & Associates Photographer, B. Durand.

Barbara Durand, partner at Durand Designs, Inc.: Private Residence, Fullerton, California, 1961. photo: courtesy, John Upton & Associates Photographer, B. Durand.

Barbara Durand, partner at Durand Designs, Inc.: Villa Samoa Condominiums, Anaheim, California, 1963. photo: courtesy, Words & Pictures, Inc. Photographer, B. Durand.

Lorraine Rudoff at William D. Coffey Associates Inc.: Banco Hopotecario de El Salvador, San Salvador, ca. 1962. photo: courtesy, Lorraine Rudoff Architectural Papers, Ms90-025, IAWA, Digital Library and Archives, University Libraries, Virginia Polytechnic Institute and State University.

Lorraine Rudoff at Albert C. Martin and Associates: IBM Manufacturing Complex, Tucson, Arizona, ca. 1979. photo: courtesy, Lorraine Rudoff Architectural Papers, Ms90-025, IAWA, Digital Library and Archives, University Libraries, Virginia Polytechnic Institute and State Univesity.

Lorraine Rudoff at Albert C. Martin and Associates: AiResearch Office Facility, Torrance, California, ca. 1982. photo: courtesy, Lorraine Rudoff Architectural Papers, Ms90-025, IAWA, Digital Library and Archives, University Libraries, Virginia Polytechnic Institute and State Univesity.

LETTER NO. 9
April 11, 1972
Northwest

1. Factors that led to architecture: I majored in art, and progressed to architecture, the "Father of all Arts." I looked for a challenge that would consume me for all eternity, and found it in architecture.

2. Professional training:
Columbia University, University of Oregon

3. I have my own practice, and work by myself, using consultants. Different types of projects: office buildings, fraternities, cooperatives, apts., small shopping center, medical clinics, post offices, fire station, restaurants, and miscellaneous.

4. Architecture is a hard profession for a woman. I am also a member of a minority race, and have known discrimination all my life.

5. Goals: to help solve some of the many social problems, to work towards better planning and design.

LETTER NO. 10
September 11, 1972
West

I am a building designer, registered with the State of California. I have no formal training in this field; my license was acquired by furnishing proof of 4 years experience through affidavits from former clients, photographs, plans, etc. I received my license in 1962 and had the required years of experience at that time.

Before then I worked in various fields of commercial art and had studied at the Layton School of Art in Milwaukee, Wisconsin. I've been an advertising artist, art editor for flight safety publications for the Air Force, and art director for three amusement parks called Santa's Village — one located in this area, one in Santa Cruz, California, and one in Dundee, Illinois. This last job involved, among other things, designing buildings, rides, etc. that would conform to the Christmas theme.

My former husband was a general building contractor, and my training and experience came through working with him. I gradually moved away from the art field into full-time building designing.

The community in which I live is a fast-growing recreation center for Southern California, with an increasing demand for permanent and vacation homes. My work is exclusively in this category — single family custom homes.

In 1964 my husband died in a plane accident, and in order to continue the construction business I applied for and received a general contractor's license. . . . Because of my position it was necessary to do the designing, bid the jobs, supervise construction, and work closely with crew and clients.

I'm no longer active as a general contractor although I have retained my license, and have remarried, but I intend to continue working as a designer as long as the demand exists.

I can make some comment regarding my clients: working in the residential field usually involves a husband-and-wife situation. I found that as a general contractor over 50% of the men were ill at ease and dubious about discussing construction with me and preferred to talk to my superintendent; none of the women had this attitude. As a building designer, I haven't detected much of that type of reaction from either husband or wife. Most of them, in fact, are enthusiastic about having a woman plan their homes. My relationship with clients is generally very good.

I also do plans for local contractors and have been told by several of them that they prefer my work to that of others in the area, all of whom are men. So I've encountered no discrimination in this regard.

My goals are simply to reflect the individuality and needs of people to the best of my ability, and to design so that the structure will be in harmony with the terrain and our mountain scene. I am as concerned as everyone else about ecological problems, and feel that our area, with its mountains, evergreens, and wildlife, should be developed with great care, and that its natural contours and resources be maintained in every possible manner. Unfortunately, such developers as Boise-Cascade have moved in and have shown a fine disregard for careful planning of land use.

In designing for our particular type of environment, I plan for maximum view in the general living areas to bring the outdoors inside visually; I use large expanses of glass, open-beam ceilings, and large roof timbers. In contrast to this, it is also my thought that there is an instinctive need for the security of intimate areas, where man can retreat from the sometimes overpowering presence of great heights of mountains and trees; these two concepts are usually kept in mind when I design, unless of course the client has a very definite idea of what he wants, which might be in opposition to this.

LETTER NO. 11
August 30, 1972
West

I sort of naturally evolved my interest in architecture. My father was a lumber dealer and when I developed a great interest in art — and a small talent — and had no difficulty with math and that sort of thing, Daddy would remark, "Wouldn't it be nice if our daughter would be an architect." Somewhere along the line the suggestion took — I certainly was never under any pressure in any form. So I went to Cornell University and received my B. of Architecture in 1959.

I practiced architecture several years — would add up to about 5 years in all, I guess. I'm really still practicing — so to speak — I read things and collect all manner of product literature, etc. My intentions are good, I've always planned on going back to work after my younger son is in first grade. The difficulty is that my husband is in the Navy so we don't always stay in one place very long — and not necessarily in a place where there are jobs. This also is limiting to any private practice I might collect — our friends are not in positions to do any building. I have designed things like decks and small remodeling ventures for neighbors. I'm also very, very rusty.

I consider myself lucky — I've always worked for small firms so I've had experience in all phases of a project. It's limited experience in a way since it was all relatively small construction. My main job was the 3 years I spent with a firm in San Francisco where one partner is an architect and the other a landscape architect. The greater share of their practice works out to be landscape work which really is a kind of micro-architecture — usually a residential type scale and more often than not involving some degree of building remodeling. Most of our straight architecture was residential; we did many garden center type things all over the country. So, on a small scale I've done it all — from surveying to attending the housewarming party. I also answered the phone, did the books, wrote checks, took a lot of pictures, ran errands, set up exhibits at garden shows and fairs and the like, interviewed potential draftsmen, went searching for new office space, and even fell in a large hole the first time I went to check a job in progress by myself.

Yes, I've been subjected to sex discrimination — it works two ways though, and on the whole I was privileged because of my sex more than the other way. Of course, that's not right either. The specific instances of discrimination I can recall occurred in Boston. As one very senior partner walked down the hall with me to meet the head of the design department he pinched me. I was offered a job too, and didn't take it. Then, when I did get a job I was horribly underpaid. It took me a while to realize it — the argument used was that I didn't have a family to support; in actual fact, I wasn't earning enough to support me. One larger thing came up then — the office was investigating Blue Cross coverage and the one single male in the office and I would have had to pay as much as anyone else. We put our feet down about that.

The good side of the discrimination issue. I learned very rapidly in college to take advantage of my sex (I don't mean that the way it sounds). One of my classmates arrived with a chip on her shoulder and a whole aura of "I'm as good as any guy and better than most." The guys didn't much like her and she was and is a marvelous girl. Anyway they resented her successes, etc. I just kind of bumbled along in my own fashion (and I'm far from being a cuddly, ultra feminine type) and asked for help when I needed it and took their teasing and when I came up with something good the guys were more pleased about it than I was. I love them all dearly and they love me and I truly don't think any of their wives are the least bit jealous or any of that sort of nonsense.

So, when I hit the real world it worked the same way. Every office seems to have one older, experienced draftsman type who'd been drawing and detailing for years. Every office I worked in these gentlemen took me under their wings and taught me all I know about such practical things. By the time I got to San Francisco I knew the traps to avoid. A friend gave me a list of firms and those that discriminated I never even bothered with — there weren't too many — and the rest of the San Francisco architects always seemed to me to be the least prejudiced group of people I've ever known. Good help was hard to come by and no one cared at all what color or sex or shape or anything a person was as long as they could do what they were hired to do.

The worst discrimination I ever faced was the interviewer I drew in the final step of my California license. As I was waiting for my turn two people told me I'd better hope I didn't get the guy that hated everybody; women, especially. So I got him. He immediately jumped to my supervision experience. I had far more of that than anyone I know who's worked for large firms only — and far more than the hot-shot designer types, etc. He asked me to describe what I would look for while inspecting a foundation. So I did — and correctly. But, when the letter came I needed to prove more supervision experience. I felt like I'd been kicked. But the reasons it was all such a shock and a mess were reasons that could be used to prove that women can't be relied on as men can. Because of my husband's job we were leaving the state in less than a month and I was 6 weeks pregnant. So what do you do? I found a friend who dragged me around all his jobs for a week and then he wrote a letter for me, so it all worked out. It was almost as if that man knew my dilemma and was out to grind me into the ground.

As for my goals — I really can't say. I want to work again; I love architecture and architects. I've also dreamed about teaching — history of architecture, perhaps. I'm intensely interested in the things being done with community involvement and neighborhood improvement and self-help type of things. If we land in a town where something of that order is established I would love to do volunteer work of that kind. Again, when you're a transient, getting something like that started is nearly impossible. Maybe I'll get lucky!

As I was writing this I realized how very personal all this is. I don't know if there's any meat here at all.

LETTER NO. 12
August 15, 1972
West

Brief History:
　　During my first years at Barnard (B.A. 1936), I considered seriously what I might do with a talent for drawing and a mathematics major. A cousin, remembering how I used as a child to draw plans with a sharp stick in the wet sand at the beach suggested Architecture. Learning of Columbia's "Professional Option" (taking the first year at any of the University's professional schools in lieu of the senior year at Columbia or Barnard, provided all qualifications of the student's major had been met by the end of the junior year), I applied for admission to Architecture and was accepted. My first year was so successful that it was settled that I would continue and take my degree (B. Arch 1939). The year at M.I.T. was sheer luxury: I was offered a full scholarship and felt it a good idea, *especially for a woman,* to have as much qualification as possible.
　　Both Columbia and M.I.T. were entirely without prejudice as far as women were concerned. In fact, I left Columbia with all the academic honors (AIA medal for general excellence, Alumni medal for design, N.Y. Institute of Archs. medal for construction) and then picked up more at M.I.T. In a sense this was unrealistic: I was totally unprepared for the shock of rejection in looking for work. I was told, for example, when asking for an interview at Skidmore's New York office, "we don't hire women." I was so taken aback that I blurted "Oh, I thought yours was a firm of *modern* architects." It was their turn to be taken aback, and I was granted an interview. *All* the top brass of the office turned out to see this brash female. They were very interested and pleasant with me, and told me they were "impressed . . . but we don't hire women!" Shortly thereafter, this ban was broken, and women have risen to very high positions in the firm, but I was there too soon: I am certain I was the first woman they ever interviewed. It was valuable experience: I had learned what I might expect. Marriage, shortly thereafter, cut short my New York office experience (before I was able to put in the office time

required for licensing exams) and I went to Canada as a bride.

Until the advent of our first child, I worked (as a civilian) with the Royal Canadian Navy, but moved, after the birth of our daughter to Britain, where for *ten years* I was a housewife, for the rather surprising reason that we couldn't *afford* the luxury of my working. Britain's taxation system at that time made it virtually impossible for me to work: as a wife, my income was considered my husband's income (!) and he was already, as Chief Architect of one of Britain's new towns, over the limit and into the supertax bracket. Supertax started at £2200 (about $6000!) and was then 19/6 in the pound, or 971/2%! This meant that if I were to earn £40 per week, I would be able to keep £1 ($4); however, as a woman I was not privileged to earn as much as a man, and my salary would have been about £5, which meant I would have netted about 30/— ($6; not $6 per hour, but *per week!*) at the same time paying more than twice that princely sum for any kind of baby-sitting, and additional for carfare, etc. My husband's position had many obligations which cost us money, but not only was there no expense account, there was no allowable tax deduction. We could not afford this luxury, and I stayed at home and produced another child.

This economic oppression was the main reason for our leaving Britain in 1955 and coming to California. Here I was not only "allowed" to work, I was required to do so, as we were starting literally from nothing, and money was needed. Starting again after such a long interval was extremely difficult; once having made this painful return, I determined not to be put off again for any reason. Thus, even the arrival of twins, several years later, did not put me off course, and I returned to work while the twins were still very small. At an advanced age, with four children (and a husband!) to look after, I took and passed my license exams, and became, at long last, "a real architect." In 1968 I started working on my own, doing everything from job-getting, client handling, designing, right down to typing my letters, sending out bills, bookkeeping, getting my own tea, vacuuming the office! With only four years of work on my own, I have not yet built up a practice to challenge that of Skidmore Owings and Merrill, but I am increasing in strength, I have happy clients, and a busy schedule. Currently I have three things going, and see this as a sign that the future holds more and better things to come.

As I have said, I have certainly felt job discrimination, but in working for myself I have enjoyed freedom from this, at least on the surface: anyone who comes to me as an architect is obviously not prejudiced against women; who knows how many *never* come because they *are* prejudiced? One eminent (male) doctor was asked recently how he would select a doctor *for himself* in a new community, without knowing anything about the local doctors. He replied, without hesitation, "I'd choose a woman." In response to the raised-eyebrow response to this statement he explained: a woman had to be good just to get into a medical school, even better to graduate and qualify, and if she's in practice with any success you can be *sure* she is superior; there are men, on the other hand, who just about squeak through.

I hope that this line of reasoning will carry over to people who are looking for an architect: the situation is much the same. Meanwhile, I work as hard as I can, all the time, sparing no pains, to justify the faith of my clients.

LETTER NO. 13
July 10, 1972
West

I am going to give you a rather lengthy history, though by no means complete. Probably it is a unique story were it compared to that of the average male architect or designer but I suspect that it is less remarkable among women who must usually be unusual to compete in a man's world.

I was born in 1929; raised in Southern California; a professional musician in my teens, 1943–47; graduated from Compton Junior College, 1947 (3 majors: Math-Science, Music, Languages); married in 1947 (my current state); began practice as a draftsman apprentice/partner to my husband, 1949 (our own business); bore two children, 1952 and 1953; became Vice Pres. . . . . upon incorporation of our successful business, 1958; licensed as a Building Designer, 1965; "retired," 1968; resumed practice in 1970.

As you may deduce, I received no formal academic training in my profession, unless you count a year of Interior Design, an auxiliary service rendered in my practice since the beginning. My original goal as a student was toward nuclear physics, the pursuit of further training in this field being the only significant example of sex discrimination thwarting my direction. My interests were so varied and broad, however, that my reaction to this frustration was by no means a bitter one.

I was the daughter of a carpenter who excelled in an era when building sash, doors, cabinets, laying floors and plying roofing was also part of the trade. A talented man, he became a building contractor who drew his own plans. Through him I became as familiar with carpenter tools as I was with pencil and brush, and with the domestic arts, I learned from my mother. I pursued none of these in school. Why should I study what I already know when there were so many fascinating unknowns to explore?

From the earliest, resistance toward my youth or sex was easily overcome after brief consultation with prospective clients. Results of my work impressed laymen and builders recognized that I knew not only design but understood their jobs, sometimes better than they. I have never acted as if being a woman is a hindrance. (It is frequently a valuable asset.) I have always been well-paid, never lacked for work nor met with job discrimination, being self-employed. I know of only a few jobs within my reach which were lost because I lacked a prestigious title.

My career has included designing over 1,000 custom residences (the largest being 8,500 square feet, selling for $680,000.00), residential subdivisions, apartment complexes, mobile home parks, small shopping centers, medical and professional buildings, commercial and industrial buildings. My services have included architectural rendering, sign design, advertising art, industrial design, die and patent drawings, landscape design, interior design and furnishing, color coordination and supervision of construction. (I have also composed lumber lists, taken bids and compiled construction estimates.) The fact that one of my favorite hobbies is carpentry and cabinet-making, that I have done painting, upholstery, etc. and had work experience in most of the building trades have all made contributions.

My work has always been guided by a conservationist philosophy. I was greatly influenced by a study of Japanese "shibusa," much as (I suppose) was Frank Lloyd Wright in his early years. My goals were to improve the world around me architecturally without noticeably disturbing nature. These goals have sometimes, but not always, been compromised according to limitations in vision of clients or codes, the restrictions of economics, or my own strength of persuasion. As I see it, it is nonetheless the architect's duty to at least try to persuade a client toward good esthetic design and environmentally-sound usage of land, as well as provide him with the most function for the least price.

Architecture, I believe, is an art requiring a social conscience. Its consequences on lifestyle should be considered not only on a basis of its individual influence (as in a home) but in its effects on groups (as in the large-scale planning of factories, office complexes, institutions, residential neighborhoods and urban design). A conscientious architect is part of his community socially in a way that makes him or her sensitive to its human problems as well as to its civic ones and he should be a leader in its growth while responding to its special tastes and traditions.

In my own case I now feel an obligation to be as great an influence as I can toward reforming a stupidly wasteful, inefficient and destructive system of resource usage and distribution which provides the evidence for some unimaginative men to proclaim us on the brink of an "energy crisis" and for others to predict environmental disaster. I believe that our public utility systems are a mess (water, power and gas) and that they could be amended in such a way as to provide us with amenities and social benefits unknown in this country today but relying on materials, technology and resources available right now. I envision a plan which could save money (in the long run and at every level), water, fuel, existing jobs and industry while creating new jobs, new industries, avert the energy crisis, erase thermal pollution, reduce air pollution (from stationary sources), and, by reducing the need for natural gas (or oil) to produce heat at the consumer level, would avail more of this cleanest of fossil fuels for use in power plants, motor vehicles, etc.

I propose using the vast quantities of waste heat which, as power-plant coolant run-off causes most of our thermal pollution, our infinite sources of industrial process heat, and borrowed heat from geothermal deposits to give us a New Commodity, HEATED WATER. It is in this simple form that heat may be transported in its original energy-form to consumers who will use it "as is" for their space-heating and hot water needs. Instead of burning fuel massively to product heat to produce electricity (wasting at least 80% of it in the process) to send to consumers so that they can convert much of it back into heat, those consumers would receive a product that needs only circulation to give them more than they now get from a complicated and expensive private arrangement.

"Hydronics" on the public scale would also make it easy to heat streets or parks or stadiums in winter and to avail home comforts more cheaply to the poor. My science background and familiarity with the growth and current application of commercial systems led me to suspect several years ago that my vision was possible. Research so far has brought me into contact with people, ideas and information which have developed my theories into convictions — have convinced me that the vision is practical.

I have only just begun to fight. Perhaps women architects are a special breed who would like to join me. (I seldom regard my place in the world, intellectually or spiritually, as a Woman but as a Human. However, in the furtherance of a worthy cause, . . . !)

Women are, and always have been, influential in residential architectural design as consumers or creative inhabitants. This is as true in industrial design where their acceptance of products is courted. Men admit to their good taste, their creativity, and their domestic superiority.

Architecture, therefore, should be crowded with women designers who not only appreciate buildings and interiors but who are responsible for producing them. Who better than the cook to design the kitchen? Who better than the mother and housekeeper to design the shelter for her children? Today women live and work with men in (almost) every nook and cranny of the world. Why should they not design it and supervise its (re)construction?

My opinion of American architecture today generally is that it has failed — failed in its responsibilities to our cities and to our environment, and that in its contemporary design it lacks quality and human relevance. Perhaps what the art and the profession could use is the humanizing effect of the feminine touch.

P.S. Personally, I look upon the sort of defiant pride I have in myself as a woman and the need to strive for achievement to overcome inequities as a spirit which will become less and less common as the quest for equal rights becomes more successful. I really fear that we shall be better satisfied with mediocrity, as men and women, when the challenge is gone.

LETTER NO. 14
July 3, 1972
West

I have been engaged in the practice of building design for about 20 years and it has been a great field for me.

I graduated from the Fort Wayne Art School, Fort Wayne, Indiana, and have taken other short courses from time to time. Back in the early days of our marriage, I made the rounds of architects' offices trying to find work, but none of them wanted to hire a woman. I finally did find work at some of the research facilities here in Santa Barbara, and worked for several years as a draftsman, artist, and technical illustrator.

When my husband's general contracting business had increased enough, I became associated with him, and we have done quite nicely together. I also work for two other general contractors now. I do almost all of the designing, site planning, working drawings, and securing building permits for our projects. Supervision on most projects is minimal. In the past we have been busy with quite a variety of projects: apartments, office buildings, residences, factories, remodeling, etc. I have a restaurant on the drawing boards now and have just started work on a Spanish style, five-bedroom home with a four-horse stable.

I feel that this field is a great one for women, especially if they can work for themselves.

LETTER NO. 15
June 30, 1972
West

At the start of World War II, I had completed just two years of college — I had chosen Engineering for the simple reason that math was my favorite (and easiest) subject.

Feeling patriotic, or possibly just looking for a good summer job, I went to work at Douglas Aircraft in Long Beach. Probably because of my math background, they gave me a two-week course in blueprint reading. They selected the top 10% of that group and sent us to their three-month course in tool design.

I worked as a tool designer until the war ended, at which time I married. The next four years were spent helping my husband through Stanford. The only kind of work I was prepared for was drafting. Fortunately I found a marvelous job with a Civil Engineer, A. T. Bennett, in Palo Alto. Years later he told me why he had hired me. The only question he asked was whether I understood quadrants. He said that I was the first applicant who sounded as though I really did understand them, and with that as a basis, he was confident he could teach me surveying.

The next four years were looking up records of survey, being transit man (woman?) on the survey team, taking field notes, then back to the drawing board, closing the traverses (he did teach me) and preparing the final maps for recordation.

During these same four years there was a woman architect who did a great deal to help me, and many other draftsmen in that area. She managed to talk some of the Stanford professors into giving night school courses covering perspective drawing, strength of materials, design and composition, and the history of Architecture.

After my husband graduated, we moved back to Southern California where he had a job. . . . I went to work for an Architect in Monrovia — again a very small office where I was able to learn a great deal. I did the structural detailing (from the Structural Engineers Calcs.), working drawings,

Electrical detailing — again working with the Electrical Engineer, and some specification writing.

After three years in the office, I decided to quit in order to complete my family. Our first daughter had been born while my husband was at Stanford (raising her while working is another complete story).

After our second daughter was born, I took one year off and sincerely tried to become the model housewife and mother. Thankfully, I have a husband who could see that housework and children were really not enough to keep me occupied. To put it mildly, I was bored to tears.

At about this time, we bought our house, and fortunately for me, the builder needed some plans drawn. I took over one of the bedrooms and converted it into a drafting room. From that day on, my business continually increased.

His sub-contractors would see my plans when they bid his jobs — they sent others — it just seemed to spread.

After a few years, I had a full time housekeeper, a part-time secretary, and two part-time draftsmen. At this point my husband insisted that I move the business into an office — which I did. I rented for two years, then we decided to build our own office.

It was called "Design Center," the tenants consisted of a Structural Engineer, Civil Engineer, Mechanical Engineer, Landscape Designer, Interior Decorator, Delineator, and last but not least, my Drafting Service.

During this period, I became an active member of the American Institute of Building Design. I have been on the board of directors for the past eleven years, and am now president of the Chapter. I also served on their Board of Examiners for the Professional Building Designer qualification.

Along the way, I took courses in Structural Engineering and Uniform Building Code. The scope of my work covers: single family residences, apartments, office buildings, industrial buildings, and convalescent homes.

To back-track, a year and a half after our second daughter was born we had our son. Now my oldest daughter is married and has a two-year old son (she had five years of college with a business major), our other daughter is a junior in college hoping to major in Law, our son is a freshman, considering dentistry.

So far, our children seem very well adjusted, much happier than most teenagers, my marriage has been — and still is — very successful.

I heartily recommend a career to any woman who can find something she truly enjoys doing. Of course, it takes a husband who understands her need to work, and one who is willing to cooperate in thousands of little ways.

I have never been subjected to discrimination in salary (or fees), job promotions, etc. due to sex. If there has been the least consideration given to sex, I think I can honestly say that in this field being a woman has distinct advantages.

LETTER NO. 16
July 17, 1972
West

Although majoring in chemistry in college, I took intensive engineering and drafting during the Second World War at Benson Polytechnic in Portland, Oregon; we received exceptional training in aeronautical, mechanical, architectural, etc. Then I worked for several years for Commercial Iron Works in Portland doing electrical wiring, piping and hull design on 500 ft. baby airplane carriers.

After the war I started architectural design in Los Gatos, California, eventually becoming a partner in a general contracting firm where I did all design and found remodel (both commercial and residential) particularly challenging and satisfying. Perhaps the most interesting job I did was a large chicken eviscerating plant in Lodi, California; this required a great deal of research.

Having always worked for myself, I have found that opportunities for high rise buildings have been scarce due to sex discrimination; however, individual large custom homes (emphasis on kitchens) have been more than plentiful and lucrative due to the fact that I am a woman. For the past eleven years I have been doing freelance design in Carmel and the Monterey Peninsula with great success. Being the only woman in our Chapter of American Institute of Building Designers has not been a disadvantage. The fellows have treated me as one of them; I have served for two terms as secretary.

Because I grew tired of the building business, at present I'm wearing a different hat as sales manager for a retirement company. My architectural training is invaluable as we are starting construction and sales are being made from blueprints at this time. Clients are constantly requesting alterations.

Lutah Maria Riggs: Vedanta Temple, Santa Barbara, California, 1956.
photo: courtesy, Robert Cleveland Photographer Progressive Architecture,
March, 1977.

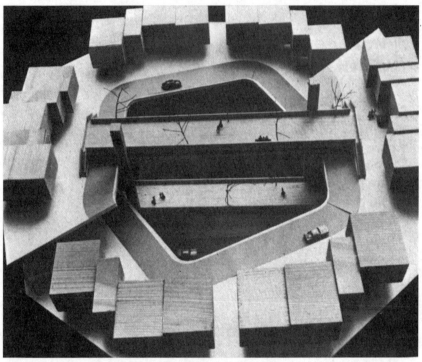

Anne Tyng: Metamorphology: Sources for Form Making, 1971.
photo: courtesy, Progressive Architecture, March, 1977.

Sarah Harkness, partner at TAC, The Architects Collaborative: Bates College
Library, Lewiston, Maine, 1971.
photo: courtesy, Progressive Architecture, March, 1977.

64

Natalie de Blois at Skidmore, Owings, and Merrill:
Equibank, Pittsburgh, Pennsylvania.
photo: courtesy, PPG Industries, Newsweek, 1977.

LETTER NO. 17
June 11, 1972
South

I should start by telling you that I was born and educated in England, where women architects are less unusual, and my comments and opinions may not be too useful. However, my background is as follows: Born 1929, London, England. Elementary, boarding, and grammar school education. One year of art study and summer in an architectural office 1946. School of Architecture, Canterbury, Kent, from 1946–1951 and passing Intermediate and Final examinations of the Royal Institute of British Architects. One year as architectural assistant in licensed architect's office as required before taking Professional Practice examination of R.I.B.A. in 1952. Assistant architectural work in Southampton office until 1953. Assistant architect position in Salisbury, England, office until 1955. Married in 1954 to an architect. Moved to Salisbury, N.C. in 1958 for husband to join architectural firm here. From 1959–1964 I had various periods of employment as desired as assistant architect, and also a period as a draftswoman in Salisbury-Rowan Planning office to familiarize myself with City and Regional planning methods and structures here. Also obtained a reciprocal license and U.S. citizenship during that time and, from small beginnings in consultation work, found an increasing number of architectural commissions coming my way. Most of them were residential, but offices and commercial work followed. Finally, when a small parochial school was offered in 1963 and we could see at least a year's work ahead, my husband and I formed our own firm. From 1964 to 1968 our office was in our home. In 1968 we took in a partner and moved the practice to downtown office space. After two years the partner formed his own practice and we have continued our firm. Thinking back, it is hard to pin down what factors led into architecture. It was not in the family so to speak, yet my twin sister is an architect married to an architect. I wanted a career that would absorb a very wide range of interests and offer a lifetime of possibilities and excitement. While looking up archaeology in a careers book, I came across architecture and virtually leaped out of the tub shouting "Eureka!" My sister did almost the same thing independently and at first we were not overjoyed by the discovery, each being a little jealous of our find. However, lack of parental enthusiasm finally made us join forces to overcome it and we went through five enjoyable and mutually sustaining years together at college. She and her husband now live and have their own practice in Perth, Western Australia.

As to discrimination I think I have probably won some, lost some. Up to the time that I was self-employed there tended to be some discrimination in salary and job promotions. However, I have always worked in relatively small private practices, where merit is the main criteria along with seniority, and it has never been a big problem. There is some individual wariness about women architects and I suppose I have felt it necessary to try harder, be more diplomatic, come through with the good idea etc., a little more than the next man might have to do. On the other hand, once into the profession women architects do have some bonuses. There is a general notion that they are bound to be good in residential work, bound to have more sensitive taste and artistic judgment, and bound to deserve more credit than males for being an architect at all. A mixed bag! I would be interested in the opinions you get about this in your studies.

My goals in architecture have been trimmed and shifted through the years, but I never did see eye to eye with Ayn Rand's concept of an architect in her book *The Fountainhead* to begin with. I prefer the now more prevalent notion that an architect is a member of a team, needing to prove a most valuable player in the construction field or else getting left out. Twenty odd years ago my goal in architecture was to be given an opportunity to practice it. "More of the same" would be the short answer today I suppose. Salisbury has a Downtown Improvement plan and an Historic Preservation Area plan. We hope that public appreciation of the renovated Community Building (1855) and adjacent mini-park will spark another drive to get them carried forward. A thriving part of our practice is in recreational developments both public and industrial, and I hope that it will continue to grow. I would like to have a hand in putting together a local break-through in the problem of low-income housing. I enjoy architecture that takes into account the way people want to live — not too tidily, having a say in things, being pleasantly surprised now and then. I have lived in large cities and small towns and it suits me very well to be in a thriving medium-sized center, with its limitations and opportunities.

To sum up, architecture has lived up to all my expectations. There are plenty of things I still want to do, like more study and research in the planning area, more travel, a survey of so called pre-historic monuments (they fascinate me with hints that our time-clock and attitude to the past might still be almost comically medieval), support improved methods of computerizing specifications, contract documents and one centralized take-off of quantities for each large project, get to hear Buckminster Fuller in person, set my own house in order, and improve my typing.

When I stop to think about it, I believe I have had large chunks of the best of several possible worlds; training that opened many doors and possibilities, interesting work and travel, marriage and five (unfashionable but rewarding) children, and a career that I hope will continue to thread itself very nicely through my life for a long time to come. There have been some tough times along the way but I really believe that architecture is a profession that many women would find most satisfying.

LETTER NO. 18
June 9, 1972
West

As for what influenced me to become an architect, I have always had some ability to draw but was convinced by my practical and conservative parents that artists were not respectable people and that was no way to earn a living. I hated the alternatives that were open to me such as secretarial work and had little ability in that area. However, I went to business school. I worked as a stenographer for a little while and then went out and joined the Marines. That was in 1942. After receiving training in radio transmission, where I was sent because of a high score in mechanical aptitude tests, I was reclassified back to stenographic work because by the time we finished training, there was no longer any need for radio operators. I did clerical work in an engineering office on the camp base where there was also assigned a woman landscape architect who was working on housing developments. I was fascinated by the work I saw her doing and decided that I could combine the things I enjoyed doing with a practical pursuit in architecture.

After I was discharged from the Marines, I went to the University of California on the G.I. Bill and graduated in architecture in 1951. I worked one summer while I was in school at the Standard Oil Co. in their engineering department to gain a little experience in drafting. The first job after graduation was very hard to find and I did encounter resentment and discrimination, some of it quite open, when I was job hunting. The economy was rather depressed then and finding a job was not easy for anyone. I finally found a job through an employment agency with the engineering department at the Bechtel Corporation. Bechtel employed several women draftsmen at that time. I was eager to get into an architectural office and when I heard that Skidmore, Owings and Merrill was hiring I went in for an interview and landed a job with that most glamorous firm in San Francisco at that time.

Meanwhile, back at the ranch, I had met a charming, talented and handsome young man at the school of architecture and we were married in 1951.

After a change in administration in Washington, SOM suddenly lost its government contracts, we were working on a hospital for Okinawa, and had to lay off large numbers of its crew. They found me a job with Vincent Rainey, who was doing a school; one of the first lift-slab jobs in this area. There was one other woman draftsman in the crew. We two and our drafting boards were installed in a large closet where we would not be able to distract the men. The whole crew was fired the day the school job was finished. There was still no work at SOM so I began to job hunt again. My husband and I were both unemployed at that particular time. He found a job and then got an offer from another small firm we all coveted so he recommended me for it. I refused to take it however when the much admired architect imposed the added requirement that I type. I could type of course, (well, I could then) and probably would have if I'd been hired first and asked later, as the men were.

Two fellows that I went to school with started their own office in a neighboring community and offered me a job. They promoted jobs, wrote the specifications and did field supervision. I did the design, renderings, working drawings of whatever they brought in including subdivision houses, schools, a mortuary, stores and offices; none of it very good. The job was fun but the commute was awful and the pay uncertain so when I heard of a job opening at the Univ. of Calif. Office of Architects and Engineers, I interviewed for it and got it. I was the first woman architect in the U.C. non-academic system. Now, there are four. I was hired as a senior draftsman but soon was given the responsibility of administering buildings constructed on campus. After I passed my certification exams, I was promoted to Project Architect and given raises at regular intervals until I reached the top of the pay scale for my classification. Until my two bosses retire, there is no chance for further advancement here. My job involves some programming for the buildings assigned to me to be constructed on the Berkeley campus; liaison between the future occupants of the building and an outside architect appointed to execute the building; coordination of the separate phases of the work such as site clearance, building construction, furnishing and landscaping; responsibility for budget; checking with reviewing agencies; time schedule; review and criticism of the outside architects' production and product; etc. In many cases, we have the opportunity and indeed the obligation to influence the design of the buildings. I work with some of the country's best known architects. . . . Until the last year or so, each Project Architect had several multi-million dollar projects going at the same time plus several smaller remodeling jobs. With the current fiscal situation, the jobs and staff have diminished to the point where we have only a few major projects and only four Project Architects (two of them women), a Senior Architect and a Campus Architect. In addition to administration, we now take a crack at some of the smaller jobs ourselves. I've done special equipment, casework projects, small remodelings and interior decoration projects all along but lately the number has increased considerably. I've recently finished remodeling and redecorating a house, designed by Julia Morgan in 1929, which the University bought for its Executive Vice President. In that particular case, I handled all phases of the architect's and decorator's work.

Your question about goals is difficult for me to answer. I am quite content with my life as it is. If my husband were offered a better job in another part of the state, I would not hesitate to leave my job but, barring that, I probably will remain where I am until I retire or am laid off. I have been doing some painting in water color and acrylics lately and am enjoying that very much also.

LETTER NO. 19
May 31, 1972
South

I was laid-off by my employer in October, 1970, because of lack of work. I worked for an Architect in San Antonio, Texas, but returned to my former employer when the work here increased.

Most of my experience has been Production and Production Administration. This is the area of architecture which I enjoy the most.

I have suffered very little discrimination in my career. I found some architects hesitant to hire women, but I found others who preferred women. One firm with whom I worked had two women architects and two women mechanical draftsmen. The firm I am currently with has employed several women, including a black woman. The most trouble I had finding employment was after I had enough experience to supervise production work, which meant men working under me. Again it was a matter of finding the right firm. In general, I feel that I get along well with the men with whom I work. As to salary and job promotions, I feel that I have received just what I have had the guts to ask for, to fight for, and to work for.

I am certain that being raised in an old-time construction family was a factor in my choice of architecture. I considered Interior Design, but happily stayed with architecture.

I find the profession frustrating but satisfying. The greatest thrill of the profession is to see something you have worked on being built. Nothing is architecture until it is built.

LETTER NO. 20
May 31, 1972
South

For myself, I am not a Texan as you have probably supposed, but was born and reared in Vermont, and after my Cornell graduation in 1917 and a couple of short jobs in Vermont, I
went to Boston. There was no architectural work to be had, and
I worked as a ship-draftsman in the Boston Navy Yard for two
and a half years, through and after World War I, then in several
architectural offices in and around Boston until 1924. Then I had
to come to Houston because my parents had moved here from
Vermont to be nearer to some of my father's business interests,
my mother had become seriously ill, and there was absolutely
no other way to meet the problem of caring for her. After her
death in 1926, I went back to Boston briefly, did some temporary
office work there then returned to Houston, where I have been
ever since. I had work in some Houston offices for a time, but
depressions and wars always hit architecture very hard. During
World War II, I again was a ship draftsman for almost the whole
4 years. Since then I have worked around Houston, mostly in
other architects' offices.

As to why I entered architecture, this goes well back into
my childhood. I wanted to be an architect as early as I found out
there were such, about the age of 9 years. I am still trying to be
one.

I have worked mostly for other architects, with a few
engineers and landscape architects, but have done some things
independently. I have my license or registration as an architect
in Texas, and am a past member of the Houston Chapter of the
American Institute of Architects. Several years ago I resigned
from that when I expected to work outside this state for some
time, and have not rejoined.

I have long had an interest in residential architecture
and worked in it, but that as a part of architecture has largely
gone, except in quite expensive houses, and in some group housing. Quantity production in speculative house building with
little architectural work involved is now common.

I have loved working in architecture. Even though some of it can be drudgery, it has its fascination. Yet for me it has meant much struggle, and required a lot of perseverance (or stubbornness). I have many times been refused jobs or opportunities because I am a woman, either by evasion or quite flatly. I have almost always been paid less than a man in a similar job, have been refused opportunities for advancement, and when work in the office drops off, and a cut in the force comes, the woman is usually among the first to be fired. The problem of getting enough work at enough money to tide over the intervals when there was no job has always been with me.

I realize that part of my difficulties have been due to the general business conditions of the period in which I have lived and worked, with its wars and depressions. Also, the whole organization of the practice of architecture has been going through changes, and more are coming.

My time has also corresponded to the great development in the recognition of women, however slow it has seemed. It is now developing rapidly, too late to do me much good, but I rejoice to see it coming. I just hope that women will be able to handle it now that they are getting it. That will not be easy to do.

LETTER NO. 21
May 18, 1972
South

In 1948 I was licensed to practice in Florida and have been in partnership with my husband ever since. No special factors in life led me to architecture unless you can say that building with blocks was my favorite play as a child. I received my Bachelor of Architecture from Columbia University, where I met my husband who is also my partner. We have a diversified practice, including schools, churches, houses, apartments, and motels. In the past, I did many of the working drawings. Now my work seems to consist of site planning, preliminaries, specification writing, and general office management.

Salary wise, I experienced discrimination in World War II when I worked for the Navy Bureau of Yards and Docks as a draftswoman. Professionally, the only real discrimination I have experienced has been in the local A.I.A. structure where I am the one of the few of my peer group who has never been asked to hold an office, head a commission, or serve as a chapter officer. Nevertheless, I have had continuous corporate membership since 1950 and intend to keep it that way.

My goals in architecture are very mundane at this point. The first priority is to restructure our practice into a diversified firm, one that is able to move with the ever-changing practice of architecture, and one that can meet any challenges that come.

P.S. November 2, 2006

Since 1972 the attitude towards women has changed, all for the better. I served as president of the Palm Beach A.I.A. chapter, and on the board of the Florida Association of the A.I.A. (now the Florida Caribbean Association). I was nominated by my chapter, and received the Hilliard T. Smith Award for Community Service, a statewide award by the Florida Association of the A.I.A. This change in attitude towards women in practice occurred when the "old guard" in the local chapter retired and a younger generation entered our profession.

The Columbia University degree of Bachelor of Architecture was changed retroactively to Master of Architecture to be in line with other schools of architecture, so I became a M. Arch. automatically.

LETTER NO. 22
March 6, 1974
Midwest

I shall begin with a resumé of vital statistics:

I. Born June 20, 1922 in Fremont, Ohio, the third child in a family of three girls and one boy. Raised through childhood and to college age in this community where my family had lived since early 1800's.

II. Family background — Father, was a general contractor for commercial, institutional, educational, and industrial buildings. Grandfather was a contractor and designer of residential work. Mother died during early childhood, and stepmother was a postmistress of ten years service when she married with two years of college. Family origin was mostly German with some English and Irish.

III. Graduated from high school in 1940 with majors in Fine Arts and Math. Had nine years of private piano lessons and five years of private fine arts lessons during secondary schooling.

IV. Entered Kent State University in fall of 1940 to major in Fine Arts (1940–1941). (My father could not see a woman in architecture, but my stepmother and his partner persuaded him to let me try the next year.)

V. Graduated Ohio State University, June 1945, with Bachelor of Architecture after doing five years in four on an accelerated war-time program.

VI. Passed Ohio Architectural Licensing exam in November of 1946.

VII. Work Record:
  A. Two summers after high school worked for a lumber company doing estimate take-offs and residential drafting.
  B. Part-time college work: 1. Two years Geodetical surveys for U.S. Geodetical Service; 2. Two years of part-time architectural drafting for Howard Dwight Smith, Ohio State University Architect.

C. First full-time job with architects in Chicago, June of 1945 thru June of 1948, June of 1949 thru February of 1950. Work included working drawings, design and specifications in residential and commercial buildings.

D. January of 1949 thru June of 1949 worked in Los Angeles, California doing design, working drawings, and specifications.

E. Began private practice in West Lafayette, Indiana in January of 1952, mostly residential design, drawings, specifications, and supervision. My office was in my home until the summer of 1966.

F. Opened separate office outside my home in 1966 until 1969 doing residential and commercial work.

G. In October of 1969, I became an Associate in a newly formed firm of consulting engineers and architects. . . . It is a small compact group of two engineers and myself, with a total office staff of 11. Half of our work is bridge and road work, and the other half is commercial, educational, institutional, and industrial building work.

VIII. Married my husband of Chicago in October of 1946. He was a teacher of languages in high school and college. We have eight children, born from 1950 thru 1962, three boys and five girls.

IX. Received Indiana Architecture License by reciprocity in 1957.

X. Community Activities: Formerly active in Catholic Church Catechism teaching, elementary PTO, and volunteer mental health auxiliary. Now active in Retarded Children's Association.

To comment on my life and work with respect to being a professional woman or "Woman in a Man's World", here are some general observations:

1. College — In a school of Engineering, I do not recall unacceptance at any time by faculty or students in my field or related engineering fields. In some instances, I believe it was to my advantage. Partly due to war-time, our classes were

small and we were closer in communication between faculty and students. My senior year, I was tutored except for one other who graduated a quarter earlier than I. At graduation, I was not allowed in the Engineering Honorary as they had never had a woman eligible before, but this never seemed of importance anyway.

2. My first job after graduation was in Chicago and after only two other interviews, I was employed. In the first place, I only selected small offices to call upon and who specialized in residential work. I did not intend to put doorknobs on doors all day long. I was most fortunate to have my boss as my first guide into the field of architecture. He was a meticulous designer, but a superb teacher and always had time to stop and discuss the design of a detail in building to fine china, furniture, or most anything. It was a small office with one partner doing business supervision, and dealing with clients leaving my boss and myself to design, working drawings, and specifications.

3. My husband and I traveled one year to the West Coast where I worked about six months with an architect in California, residential design. I did pound the pavement there, visiting over 100 offices before finding a job. A few would not even interview women, but most were very cordial.

4. It was very fortunate for me and my growing family that my profession could function reasonably well in a home situation. I still do not approve of women with small children working completely away from their families constantly. I realize in some cases it is a virtual necessity.

5. After several years of private practice in my home, my children were finally all in school. I then opened an office in West Lafayette. My business more than doubled the first year, and I started doing a great deal of office and commercial building as well as residential.

There may have been times when I was not selected as an architect or even considered because I was female. I really preferred residential work which a good many architects do not touch anymore. Nonetheless, I probably developed a great deal of recognition as an architect doing homes where I was able to meet more people, particularly business men who then came back for their commercial or other work.

Since I have joined a group now, I no longer have quite the burden of a private practice where I was designer, draftsman, secretary, bookkeeper, supervisor, et cetera.

I still believe over half the battle of women doing anything is their own self-esteem. If one feels qualified and even better than the next man or woman, many problems are wiped out.

LETTER NO. 23
September 15, 1973
East

I enclose a copy of a short piece my mother wrote several years ago, "An Architecture Co-ed 'Way Back When'," and may have sent to someone at Cornell.

Mother used to comment that the thing she was most interested in, houses, was not regarded as very important for an architect in comparison to designing monumental gateways or pavilions for fair grounds.

Anyway, she did design two houses — for herself and our father in Lafayette, Indiana, and for the family of five plus her parents in Washington. Other than this any direct application of her training was frustrated by marriage and a family.

Nevertheless, I am certain that her lifelong interest in architecture, and her opportunities to see examples ranging from English cathedrals to houses by Frank Lloyd Wright, was a constant pleasure and satisfaction to her.

An Architecture Co-ed 'Way Back When'

> In the fall of 1901 our class entered the College of Architecture at Cornell, a dozen or so raw freshmen with one thing in common: the desire to study Architecture. In the big freshman drafting room on the second floor of Lincoln Hall we made our start, drudging through the Orders, through Analytics and through History of Architecture and hoping that all this was somehow getting us somewhere.
>
> The boys, I am sure, were dismayed and not much pleased to find a girl in the class but they were always tolerant and polite, even the boy who didn't think much of women, anyway. I kept myself to myself and tried to be inconspicuous.
>
> A dozen of us started; nine finished the course with a good number of Second Medalists among us.

By the time we were in our sophomore year we were getting used to each other. By the time we had finished Second Year Design we began to see what it all might be about. And when we entered Junior Year, with its agonies of Mechanics, Bridge Design and Details of Construction, we were a close little community and the "strong-minded co-ed" was accepted as part of it, which was rather gratifying.

Our quarters included only the east end of Lincoln. The west end was occupied by the Civil Engineers who were regarded by us as a lower order of beings, serious minded and sordid, caring only for their studies, and were hailed with contempt as "Plumbers!" They retaliated with "Carpenters"; since they considered us a frivolous bunch, impatient of set times for work and even bursting into song at our drafting boards.

Certain time-honored traditions held in the College. On St. Patrick's Day green and orange bunting was draped impartially from the windows, symbols which the engineers were eager to tear down. A new faculty baby's arrival was greeted with a long list of names on the blackboard from which the parents were supposed to choose. I don't remember that they ever did.

Now and then a water trap was arranged on the top of the door to the senior drafting room, then some unwary under-classman was invited to come in for consultation on his own work. One day Dean Clarence Martin arrived before the student did and received the whole bucket full on his head. For a moment the class was petrified but he was a good sport and passed it off with a smile.

Senior year went by happily. We were by now a democratic group ranging from the boy who had made his own way since a lad to the son of a wealthy brewer, with the rest of us in between. Work was often a community affair. If someone was behind with his final drawings there was always a friend to step in and help with the inking in or the rendering. When I tipped over a bowl of dilute ink on my nearly finished elevation there were half a dozen bowls of water ready instantly to wash it off before serious damage was done. I think a good bit of the water went into my lap.

Our singing was something rather special. Visitors to the Campus were brought past our windows to "hear the architects sing." The bunch obliged with their special renderings of "Beulah Land" or "The Sweet By-and-By," both of these offering great opportunities for close harmony and improvisations, sometimes I grieve to say, of an irreverent character. There were also some impromptu anthems, devised as the spirit moved. "The Lost Dividers" and "All Policemen" with antiphonal responses were most impressive. All the boys were more or less musical. One had been a "boy-soprano" and had a high clear tenor. Another knew music well and was for two years the official "Chimes-smasher". I think all could at least carry a tune, even the class "oracle" who always knew all the answers.

From the more social meetings of the class or the College I kept aloof. When Christmas came and the Seniors put on the traditional Christmas Tree for the College, I think the boys were worried that I might want to be there. I allayed their concern by stating that I would not come, but would like to furnish the candy bars for the tree. For a week my room-mate and I at Sage College spent our study time making dozens of gay little tarleton bags and pounds of fudge, taffy, and French bon-bons. They really made a great hit and next morning I found on my table a book I had long wanted and a note from our Professor of Design, Maurice Prevost — "vos bon-bons sont vrai bons!"

The College was a simpler place sixty years ago. They are better quartered now, more students and a bigger faculty, as well as a greatly expanded program. But we feel sure that the old ideals still hold — loyalty to the profession, joy in one's work and a gay spirit for both work and play.

LETTER NO. 24
February 9, 1973
Northwest

This is a note to introduce myself as a licensed and practicing female Architect. Our National A.I.A. office somehow still has me listed as a "Mr." Perhaps it is computer reluctance.

L. Jane Hastings: Addition and Remodeling for Terry Thompson Residence, Seattle, Washington, 1961. photo: courtesy, Photograph by Hugh N. Stratford, L. Jane Hastings Architectural Papers, Box 2, Ms2004-004, IAWA, Digital Library and Archives, University Libraries, Virginia Polytechnic Institute and State University.

L. Jane Hastings: David J. Quam Residence, Seattle, Washington, 1968. photo: courtesy, L. Jane Hastings Architectural Papers, Box 1, Ms2004-004, IAWA, Digital Library and Archives, University Libraries, Virginia Polytechnic Institute and State University.

L. Jane Hastings: N. J. Johnston Residence, Seattle, Washington, 1975.
photo: courtesy, L. Jane Hastings Architectural Papers, Box 2, Ms2004-004,
IAWA, Digital Library and Archives, University Libraries, Virginia Polytechnic
Institute and State University.

Emily V. Obst, partner at Obst Associates Architects / Planners Inc.: Skyer Residence, West Palm Beach, Florida, 1960. photo: courtesy, E. V. Obst.

Emily V. Obst, partner at Obst Associates Architects / Planners Inc.: New Pool and Building Addition to Chapin Residence, West Palm Beach, Florida, 1965.
photo: courtesy, E. V. Obst.

Emily V. Obst, partner at Obst Associates, Architects / Planners Inc.: Mangonia
Residence, Elderly Housing, West Palm Beach Housing Authority 1988.
photo: courtesy, E. V. Obst.

LETTER NO. 25
February 11, 1972
East

I have worked one way or another in the field since I graduated from M.I.T. in 1919, first as draftsman-designer in the office of Grosvenor Atterbury, N.Y.C., then in my own practice.

As for what led me to the profession: When I was studying design in the Boston School of the Museum of Fine Arts I found that the work, though highly interesting and delightful (we practically lived in the Museum) seemed to lead toward a career in interior decorating — the early form, largely providing rich clients with expensive lamps and sofa coverings.

So my father, an architect, encouraged me to go to M.I.T., his own school.

My main interest has been in housing designed for low-income families, as you will see from the Vita.

I have been fortunate, as the timing coincided with the growth of government's interest in housing.

Vita

B.S. in Architecture, Mass. Institute of Technology.

New York Registration.

Private practice, New York based, 1931–1942. Estate work, country houses, N.Y. City alterations. Medal, "Better Homes in America" competition, 1933.

A.I.A. Langley Award, 1937-'39, for study of housing for low-income families. Report published in *A.I.A. Octagon* Oct.-Nov. 1941; also briefed in *Architectural Record* 1943, and translated in full in *La Habitacion Popular*, govt. publication in Argentina.

War emergency appointment, Fed. Public Housing Authority, 1942.

Edited *Public Housing Design*, experience manual, Govt. Printing Office, 1946.

Principal Project Planner in Design Department, N.Y.C. Housing Authority, 1947-'62. Acted as liaison between Authority and architects under contract. Edited, with continuing revisions, *Memo to Architects*, handbook of Authority procedures, requirements, and technical experience.

1963 to date: Architect / Consultant: to Public Housing Administration and to semi-public and private organizations.

Author, *Family Living in High Apartment Buildings*, commissioned by P.H.A., Govt. Printing Office, 1965.

European travel and study, 1924, '35, '55, '62, '66, '70, and '71; also to Egypt, part of Middle East, Mexico, Puerto Rico, West Indies, and Canada.

Paris agent to assemble and ship collection of paintings and art objects, the nucleus of the Fitchburg, Massahusetts Art Museum.

Committee work: American Public Health Assoc., Community Service Society, Citizens' Housing and Planning Council, New York Chapter, and national organization of A.I.A.

Organized and conducted first course of lectures and demonstrations in home repairs for American Women's Voluntary Services, 1942.

Member, Landmarks Preservation Commission of N.Y.C., 1970.

Author of numerous technical articles and book reviews in professional journals, and articles on housing in newspapers and home magazines.

Listed in *Who's Who* and *Who's Who in Architecture*.

Citation on the occasion of the centennial celebration of Wilson College, Chamersburg, Pa., March 22, 1969.

A.J. Thomas Award for Pioneer in Architecture, New York Chapter, A.I.A. June 1969.

LETTER NO. 26
May 16, 1972
South

There is some question in my mind exactly how to convey the information. Since my life, at least for the past 23 years, has been so involved with architecture, it is difficult to separate the facts from the feelings, and in my case, I believe that feelings are of equal importance.

Why Did I Study Architecture?

That is a question that I have been asked dozens of times. I can only speculate as to the many underlying forces that directed my choice. My first memory of thinking about architecture was in the last year of high school when I was deciding what to study in college. I remember there seemed to be two choices: art or architecture. My mother said at the time — "You become an architect and show them how houses should be designed" (for the women who use them). I got the feeling that my mother wanted me to succeed in a man's field – engineering, law, medicine (nursing was *not* an acceptable choice) or architecture. But, on the other hand, she felt my goal in life was to be a wife and mother — the only reason to get an education was to have something to fall back on in case something happens to your husband. (Art was therefore not as acceptable as architecture.)

My father's influence was a little different. I don't remember his ever actually saying anything, but the motivation was more compelling. I subconsciously needed to achieve to gain my father's love. I was his "son".

On my own part, I felt I didn't have enough talent to really study art, and since art was present in architecture, I chose architecture.

During the spring of my sophomore year, I felt that I was not doing well enough in Architecture, and went to the Testing and Guidance Center to take some tests to find out if I should change majors. The counselor, after going over the tests, said there wasn't enough indication that I should change so I stayed in Architecture.

Professional Practice

During most of my professional practice, while in other offices as well as my own, I have done the detailing part of working drawings. Right after school I did some design, and delineation, as well as model building. In our office, the work was divided more or less to where my husband did the client contact, supervision, specifications, design, structural, mechanical, and some delineation. I did the architectural part of working drawings, bookwork, and some structural. Our main projects are industrial, commercial. We have done a couple of churches, schools, and a few residences. I have always worked "semi-full-time." When we have to get out the working drawings for a project, I have worked 12–14 hours a day 7 days a week for the 2 or 3 weeks required. Then a 6 hour day at other times. There was no question as to who ran the business. There were occasional conflicts on matters of design, usually of a minor nature.

Discrimination

I don't remember meeting outright discrimination in school (besides the exclusion from the Sphinx Club which I didn't expect to get in because it was male only) I was pleasantly surprised that I was even considered. Harwell Hamilton Harris became director of the school during my 4th year. I felt that he treated me as an equal (to the male students).

In our job-hunting in Dallas, after graduation, when I was told they didn't hire women . . . it really didn't bother me. Jobs were hard to get then, and we looked a long time before lucking out and both being hired by the same firm. The boss's wife was also in the office (running the office part, not the drafting), and I thought this may have had some bearing on our being paid the same wage. At other offices where I worked, I never thought about what my wage was compared to others. In El Paso . . . there were two other women architect graduates as well as two other women draftsmen. This was an office that employed about 20–25 people. I felt our status was lower, but it is hard for me to separate my own defensiveness from actual facts.

The discrimination that affected me most was in Ft. Worth in 1958. I feel the reason, partially was an ambivalence present. I felt I needed to earn the money to supplement family income, and yet, I wanted to nurse my baby and therefore, didn't want to work full-time. (Although, I never even got that far in my interview). As I see it, I was vulnerable due to a conflict in roles; and the rejection of myself as a female (my competence wasn't even investigated) brought back the original feelings of being rejected as a female by my father.

In 1966, my husband and I decided to join the AIA as corporate members. At that time we had been in practice for 5 years. We had not joined before because my husband felt the benefits would not overcome the expense, and also he did not agree with some of their policies. We were both turned down. There seemed to them to be some question of ethics involved —that we were involved in the manufacture of a building product. (We were *not*.) We had developed a tilt-wall system in conjunction with a contractor, but we were not part of his company in any way. We felt this was just an excuse. My husband did not wish to go into the matter at the time. I felt that I had not been considered on my own merits. Later I learned that I had two strikes against me. The chairman of the membership committee also did not think women should be admitted. Later, I had a friend who was a member intervene and explain the situation, and my husband's application was reconsidered. I did not ask to be reconsidered at this time because I was trying to disassociate myself from architecture.

When I entered TCU in Sociology, I found prejudice against women in that field also. In one of my courses, I did a research paper on "Working Women" and discovered that the discrimination that women do meet in regards to wages, etc.

Motivation

Since architecture and my marriage have been so intertwined, it is impossible for me to separate my personal problems from those related to architecture. I feel that some of the problems I have in interpersonal relationship are also connected to the motivation that led to my decision to study architecture. Being an architect is difficult for me, but I have invested too much of my life and self to be able to disassociate completely from it.

In regard to being my father's "son" — a story was often told in the family about an incident that occurred when I was 3 years old. I had long blond curls at the time, and a cousin was instructed to take me to get my hair trimmed (by the barber — a family friend). I climbed up into the chair and announced that I wanted my hair "cut just like my Daddy's" – which he did. Afterwards, I insisted that my name was 'Tommy' and would not answer to my own name. (The only people who call me Tommie today are my parents, sister, brother-in-law, and one Aunt and Uncle.) My name is different and has always called for comment — all my teachers throughout school had difficultly pronouncing it.

Other factors that may have influenced my decision to "work after marriage" and achieve are related to the roles my mother and maternal grandmother (who lived with us after I was six until I left home) played. During World War II, when I was about 12 or 13, my mother took a course at the University and got a job at the State Highway Dept. She did soil testing in the Testing Materials Lab. She was the only woman working in that capacity. (The only woman, other than secretaries.) My maternal grandmother owned a grocery store and ran it alone (after my grandfather died) until she was 75.

Personal Problems

I went to an interview for a teaching position at the School of Architecture at UTA. The Chairman's genuine interest and acceptance of me (being female did not concern him exactly) was quite different from my usual reception. When he asked what I had done since I left school, first, I said, that I had a family; then associated with my husband in an office. I feel that my experience in the office has been inadequate. I can't separate my own feelings (of feeling inadequate) from what I believe to be a realistic appraisal of my experience. When I started to fill out the personal data form (apply for the position) and came to "membership in professional organizations," this angry feeling surged up — a frustration that I feel I am constrained by my role, discriminated against because I am a woman, and yet, should have the wherewithal to persevere.

LETTER NO. 27
April 4, 1972
East

My wife has turned your letter over to me to answer because I am adept at the typewriter although rather inaccurate. This will be a first draft uncorrected letter which would never be written were I to take the time for a finished presentation.

My wife inherited her interest in architecture from her architect father who was a practicing architect in New York City for many years, Dean of Architecture at Cornell circa 1900–1905 and critic at the School of Architecture Columbia University. After graduating from Vassar 1925 she got her degree in architecture at Columbia and her masters in architecture from M.I.T. in 1930. She received various awards while in school which are listed in *Who's Who of American Women.*

My wife worked in her father's office after graduation and eventually was taken in as a partner. During the Great Depression when architecture was dead as a doornail, she clerked in Macy's and Wanamakers [former NYC department store] eventually getting commissions from an architect for renderings (Abutments to George Washington Bridge among others); W.P.A. came along and she got architectural work there, eventually shifting over to Civil Service in the New York City Dept. Hospitals and Public Works where she was principally a renderer. She attended the Art Students League in New York and became a member of the American Water Color Society.

During World War II she attended courses in tool design at Yale (we had moved to New Haven 1938) and then took a job as tool designer in a war plant utilizing the math for the first time in which she majored at Vassar. At the end of the war she returned to Architecture in New Haven as a designer working on many Yale University buildings, large telephone buildings, churches, and projects beyond count.

In 1958 she opened her own office in New Haven and in private practice designed and supervised quite a number of private homes, redesigned the interior of the old Seaman's Church Institute in New York, worked on the Gesell Institute in New

Haven and performed numerous alterations.

Spanning her last years as an employee and the early years of her own practice she served as delegate to the A.I.A. to various congresses in South America. She is fluent in Spanish. When that congress met in Washington in 1965, she was chairman of a large committee called the Themes Committee which read, translated, and mimeographed the many papers submitted by members for discussion (i.e. The Pan-American Federation of Architectural Societies).

My wife has never complained about discrimination. If it has been present she has been unaware of it. She is capable of performing all functions of an architect from initial sketches, working drawings, to picking out building materials, writing specs and supervising on the job. She has formed warm friendships with many contractors and though inclined to have competitive bids has a private list of builders with whom there exists a mutual trust so that she can go ahead on a cost plus basis. Contractors respect her and never more than once try to put anything over on her.

I retired in 1969 and my wife closed her New Haven office the following year. This is because we both share an interest in cruising on our sailboat and are away from home most of the summer. However, she is currently designing a house the contract for which was let a month ago. She plans to supervise till we leave for our summer sailing.

LETTER NO. 28
February 11, 1972
South

In order that I not appear to be sailing under false colors I shall say at the outset that I am not an architect.

After graduation I went into business with my father who was practicing architecture in Washington, D.C. We had been together only a short time when my father was appointed Municipal Architect for the District of Columbia. For the next five years I ran his private practice, which was devoted almost entirely to university buildings and better quality residences.

The residences were largely my responsibility. It was I who met with the clients, discussed their wants and needs and made preliminary sketches. In many cases I carried the work on to conclusion, working drawings, full size details and superintendence. In all this I never claimed to be an architect. My drawings were always signed as a designer.

I think that answers your question concerning how I used my professional training. At the end of five years I married and devoted the next ten or more years to raising a family. All the while I felt secure in the knowledge that I had professional training and experience which would enable me to hold a job should I ever wish to. In the depth of the Depression, 1932, when a job would have filled a real need, the architects were walking the streets looking for work just as I was. I never went back to an architect's office.

However, during the course of my married life, my husband and I built three houses, two of which we sold. We lived in the third one until we retired. During the war I started to teach art on a temporary basis in the public school, and remained for twenty years.

My training and experience in architecture has had a continuous influence on my life. Even in my teaching I found myself doing projects that teachers with more conventional training could not have done. One small example — when on one occasion a large steel frame building was being erected in clear view of my classroom windows, I took it as an opportunity to explain to the class how modern steel and concrete construction made possible a whole new method of building, different from conventional construction where walls supported a roof. It helped the youngsters to see why modern buildings must look different.

In my travels I find it amusing to drive through a community and read its history, as set forth in its architecture. In earlier times appreciation and skill in architecture were attributes of a gentleman, such as Thomas Jefferson. Today our world might be a happier one if women as well as men emulated this ideal.

Women, I believe, are eminently suited to the practice of architecture, and not only in the residential field. Architecture requires an original and innovative mind. Women have this to a great degree. It also demands many face-to-face relationships. Women are frequently outstanding in this area.

LETTER NO. 29
February 7, 1972
East

First, I did graduate from M.I.T. in the Class of 1916 with a B.S. in Architecture, but by no means was I one of the first women to receive a degree in Architecture from M.I.T. I cannot tell you the number that may have preceded my time, but two women who practiced architecture in Boston under the name of Howe & Manning [Doris Cole, *The Lady Architects: Howe, Manning and Almy, 1893–1965*; Midmarch Arts Press, NY] were very successful, especially in domestic work, and practiced from about the 1890s through the first half of this century until some time in the 1960s. Miss Lois Howe was made a Fellow in the A.I.A. and died several years ago at just short of 100 years of age. Miss Eleanor Manning was considerably younger and was married late in life, but I cannot now recall her married name, but the Alumni Assoc. could no doubt give it to you.

There was another girl in my class at M.I.T. who graduated in Architecture in 1916, who soon thereafter married an earlier MI.T. graduate, but she had seven children and never went on with her profession.

From childhood I had always been interested in architecture and was fortunately encouraged in this interest. After graduation I taught various architectural subjects at a school of landscape architecture — the Lowthorpe School of Landscape Architecture for Women in Groton, Mass. Besides teaching I took all the courses that dealt especially in landscape architecture that would be useful, and soon after started a practice of Architecture and Landscape Architecture in Boston. However, my interest in the Lowthorpe School carried on for many years and at various times I continued to give some of my time there to teach architectural and landscape architectural subjects.

I was especially interested in the great need to bring the architectural and landscape professions closer together, realizing how necessary it is for both professions to coordinate in the development of their programs from the very start, beginning with the study of the site and consideration of what it has to offer for the best development of the program. The knowledge and experience of the Landscape Architect is most necessary at the start of a program for the best results in the development of the buildings, but not until recent years, and sometimes not even now, has the architectural profession, on the whole, recognized the importance of this. Building design and building layout which recognizes and is integrated with the forms of land, vegetation, prospects, exposure, etc. has a better chance for success. There is still much to be done along this line and this is why I mention it especially.

My practice through the years included both architectural and landscape projects and was almost entirely given to domestic work. Being knowledgeable in both professions I was able to demonstrate in my own work the value of a very close consideration of the two fields working together.

Eventually, after the second World War, the Lowthorpe School became affiliated with the Rhode Island School of Design and became their Department of Landscape Architecture in 1945. From then until my retirement in 1965 I divided my time between my private practice in Rhode Island and the position of Chairman of the Department of Landscape Architecture at the Rhode Island School of Design in Providence where there also is a Department of Architecture so that, by some teaching in both Departments, my efforts at coordination and understanding between the two professions could bear fruit.

I am both a Member of the A.I.A. and a Fellow of the American Society of Landscape Architects.

Beverly Willis: Pacific Points Condominiums, Pacifica, California, 1972. photo:
courtesy, Beverly Willis Architectural Papers, Ms92-019, IAWA, image available
through VT ImageBase (http://imagebase.lib.vt.edu/), housed and operated by
Digital Library and Archives, University Libraries; scanning by Digital Imaging,
Learning Technologies, Virginia Polytechnic Institute and State University.
photo: courtesy, Joshua Friewald and Del Carlo Photography.

Beverly Willis: San Francisco Ballet Building, San Francisco, California, 1982.
photo: © Pete Aron/Esto, courtesy B. Willis.

Beverly Willis: Goeglien Pool House, Yountville, California, 1988.
photo: courtesy, Christiansen Photography, B. Willis.

Joan Goody, partner at Goody, Clancy & Associates: Heritage Gardens Elderly
Housing, Winthrop, Massachusetts, 1974.
photo: courtesy, Progressive Architecture, March 1977.

Joan Goody, Heaton Court Elderly Housing, Stockbridge, Massachusetts, 1978.
photo courtesy, © Clemens Kalisher Photographer, J. Goody.

Joan Goody, Wheeling Federal Courthouse, Wheeling, West Virginia, 2004.
photo: courtesy, © Anton Grassl Photographer, J. Goody.

LETTER NO. 30
February 8, 1972
East

Your letter to my mother was picked up by my brother who lives nearby. Our mother died in 1969 at the age of 86.

My mother specialized in landscape architecture at MIT. I have often heard her say that she enjoyed the study of plants and especially her work with Mr. Jack at the Arnold Arboretum, and felt more secure in this work than in architecture. She was very much interested in how plants grow if not trimmed and was keenly aware of differences in color and texture.

After MIT in 1904 she worked for two years with Warren Manning on the Jamestown exposition in VA. Then she married in November 1906 and did not practice or work for pay again.

She used her knowledge of plants as curator of the Herb Society of America and as a developer of HOSTA plants. Both of these associations she very much enjoyed.

LETTER NO. 31
February 6, 1972
East

You asked how I got started on such a difficult career? I was always drawing and loved pictures; so I thought I wanted to be an Artist. But my Father knew few artists were paid or valued until they died, when if good artists their works would be snatched at the lowest figure by those in business and sold at fabulous prices. This is all too true. He had also read *Looking Backwards* wherein the heroine was an Architect, and he believed women had never been fairly treated so I was willing and anxious to go to the M.I.T. as the best school. We lived a stone's throw from the Great Pacific Museum in Honolulu.. Father came home early one day to tell me that two M.I.T. professors were visiting the Museum — I better meet them. I lost no time and learned that I had better hurry for the M.I.T. was going to close the doors to women. In 1906 I went to be with my sister where I attended lectures by John Galand Howard eminent Architect and watched the building under construction for Engineers — at the University of California where I spent a good deal of time on the tennis courts. Two years later I was at the M.I.T. Course IV Architecture even taking charcoal drawing in Life Class. In higher mathematics I got Calculus — and after an examination that I thought I had failed I went at once to the office of Dean Burton. He said "I'm sorry. If you have failed that, there isn't much you can do going on." But I hadn't failed at all. In fact I did pretty well. And yet in the years since I have never used Calculus. So I graduated with a B.S. from the M.I.T. In September, after vacationing in Nova Scotia, and eager to have a job — I was taken on at Carrere & Hastings, then building the New York Public Library at 42nd Street; was sent to that Library on trial under Jack Humpheries and then sent to their office at 225 Fifth Ave, 12th floor. There I laid out a coffered ceiling for the Belmonts; a stone cornice for one of the Gould's houses on Fifth Ave. and a lot of lattice for the Alfred I. du Pont house. In those days all the big Architects had lunch at Mouquin's on Fifth Ave where anything new was discussed. Years later I was for a time at Magonial's who remembered the day I was taken on by Carere & Hastings — and added "I think they never had a reason to regret it." At Magonial's I laid out the ceiling for the Nebraska Library, a twin building to honor the War heroes. While Magonial liked the design, he noted I had no notion it required ventilation and suggested how it should be incorporated. After this I was taken on at several high class offices dong residential work. But that was after spending a year in Rome measuring a few palaces and loggias and including color notes. Thirteen of these drawings and color notes were on exhibition at the Architectural League when I got back to New York. In Rome I was invited to a reception at the American Academy and later to lunch with Mr. Stevan who was the director of the Academy. Once the students asked Mr. Stevan if I might have lunch with them. He replied "Certainly — she is studying Architecture."

I met Julia Morgan and she took me along while inspecting several residences. Julia Morgan built the beautiful Amphitheater for the University of California.

The greatest American Woman Architect so far as I know was Miss Julia Morgan of San Francisco. She attended and graduated from the Beaux Art in Paris. While she took her examinations the men kept on chanting "Miss Morgan, Miss Morgan" hoping to give her a hard time. This is worthy of being in your book in contrast to what it is now.

LETTER NO. 32
September 1, 1971
Midwest

The saga of my life — family tree researcher. Went thru Central Lake, Mich. high school average 98+. At 13 years planted and harvested beans for C. L. canning factory. At 14 picked beans in large field. At 15 and 16 got special permit to work in factory. Graduated at 17 and went to Charlevoix to wait tables to earn money for college. Mother moved to Ypsilanti and my sister and I worked for our board and room. Got a Life Certificate for teaching at Eastern Mich. 1911. I taught 3 years but realized it was not for me. Mother had moved to Ann Arbor so I went there, caring for a 21-room house for a living. I went to Univ. of Michigan for 4 years. I wanted to study art and mathematics and the Dean of the Lit College said I was crazy but to go to the Dean of Architecture. He said "we don't want you but since the school is co-educational and state owned we have to take you if you insist." I took all the requirements and all I wanted, now maintaining I was the first member of Women's Lib. I waited tables summers for clothes, tuition, and books. I joined the Eastern Star and Arch. honorary fraternity, Tau Sigma Delta. I graduated in 1920 with just under a B+ average.

During the first World War, I left school and worked for Dodge Bros. in Detroit, the first woman as engineering draftsman. All the boys in my class came back and we were together again. I was the first woman to receive a degree from the college of Arch. and the first person to have a daughter graduate from the same school. In 1970 my granddaughter graduated and we were three generations. I joined the Emeritus Club.

Women were not accepted in architecture but after many interviews in Chicago I was the first woman to be hired as draftsman by Perkins, Fellows & Hamilton, who gave me all-around experience.

In Jan 1921 I married but continued to work as he was in school. I quit my job Dec. 1, 1923 and my daughter was born 1-1-1924. A friend suggested I take the State Boards and I was lucky to pass the first time. I have been in private practice ever since. My son was born 12-14-1926

In 1929 I went back to work and have been the support of my family since. Social worker, employment interviewer, and architect for Illinois Labor Dept. At times I worked two jobs besides my own practice. I designed the Woman's Booth for the 1932 Chicago World's Fair. I received an award from the Builders Society of Chicago for the best design of a house on the North Shore.

LETTER NO. 33
January 16. 1972
Midwest

Since my family tree is out and you can see by my history, I will be 80 years old July 26, 1972, however I have never thought of age. I quit the State of Illinois at age 73, took 2 years to go around the world. To admit years seldom occurs to me. But I am in practice at present.

The (definition) of women in architecture is "men." One of my jobs with the State of Illinois ran close to $500,000 remodeling a large office and I had no trouble with workmen on the job or contractors. In fact many have come back to see me when they found I was supervising. One thing I found when traveling around the world — all other countries respect a professional woman and when I did discover this — I played up my profession and got red carpet treatment from Stockholm to Sydney.

I have been "hampered" in a way as I have been the sole support of my children since 1929. As to your questions — I think all are answered in the enclosed material — although I invite you to write more. The one on today's architecture would have to have a qualified answer. (I lean to traditional but can enjoy modern). But, for instance, the other day I saw a high-rise design for seniors and it was absolutely horrible — nothing but a maze, it would baffle an astronaut. They need more women in architecture and more women should insist on getting out and supervising.

I might tell you I am not a member of A.I.A. as I have always been so busy I could not attend meetings. I really feel I should be invited to be an F.A.I.A., how's that for an ego.

LETTER NO. 34
January 25, 1973
West

Having worked in a period when the United States was engaged in two world wars with a "great depression" in between, my experience is rather heterogeneous.

In 1916 I graduated from Washington University, St. Louis, Missouri with a degree of B.S. in Architecture (meaning all engineering courses were taken in the school of Engineering). I was one (only girl) of seven to graduate out of a freshman class of thirty.

I took a course in City Planning at Wisconsin in 1920 and again in 1950 at the University of California (Berkeley). I have taught Interior Design at both the High School and College levels. I also taught map drafting at the Aeronautical Chart Plant, relocated in St. Louis during the war.

During World War I, I was employed by the St. Louis City Planning Commission -Harland Bartholomew Engineer. I designed and estimated the Civic Center and several parks and playgrounds. I also estimated the cost of street widenings as well as illustrating various Commission Reports. Then in 1923 I left City Planning to return to architecture. I worked for various St. Louis architects doing mostly church architecture. During the depression I had an opportunity to do some display work and some teaching. Through my teaching I was able to establish a small business in Architecture and Interior Design. I was a licensed architect in Missouri until recently.

In 1941 I returned to the St. Louis City Planning Commission as special assistant to Mr. Bartholomew to design and execute a scale model of the City of St. Louis. This model reflected the accomplishments of the past 25 years of City Planning and showed projects contemplated for the next 25 years.

World War II was in progress so I went to work for "Uncle Sam" first with the Army Engineers then transferred to the Air Force where I taught map drafting and plotted air fields all over the world.

My next move was to San Francisco where I secured a position with the U.S.A. Building Services Division designing and furnishing U.S.O. Clubs in 5 Western states. Having performed these projects to the best of my ability I was made an Associate Director of U.S.O. Building Services-Western Division.

World War II having concluded causing the closure of many U.S.O. clubs I was again forced to seek new work. In 1946 I went to the office of Henry H. Gutterson F.A.I.A. in San Francisco acting as job captain on multi-functional and residential projects. This proved to be one of my most rewarding experiences.

In 1950 I again left architecture and became Senior Redevelopment Planner for the Redevelopment Agency of the city and county of San Francisco. In this position I was in charge of the drafting room, responsible for the coordination of utilities in the area, made a block-by-block survey and established the possible boundaries of the area. I also explained the redevelopment process to individuals and to groups.

1954 found me in Southern California where I have worked in temporary positions with several architectural firms. I retired in 1958 and have only done a few small jobs since.

I am sorry I have no pictures of my work. All I have are some pamphlet reproductions and some glass plates (early color slides) of an interior. In my day I didn't have to submit samples of my work and present a resumé as they do today. I just walked in and asked for a job. In 1928–30 I was national president of what is now Association of Women in Architecture.

LETTER NO. 35
1972
West

Now about A.W.A. (Association of Women Architects). A brochure is enclosed — just a short description of background etc.. We were national at one time but interest lagged, few women were studying architecture and fewer were joining our group. Only the Los Angeles chapter remains. Mae Steinmesch one of the founding members (in 1917 on the steps of Washington University, St. Louis) is a member of our chapter. There is a possibility of a chapter at U.S.C. — I meet with the girls tomorrow. Dolores Hayden was a recipient of one of our scholarships; we award at least 2 each year. I believe the brochure covers most everything.

LETTER NO. 36
June 20, 1972
West

I am sorry to delay so long in acknowledging your letter regarding your research on women in architecture. Hopefully this information will not be after-the-fact!

1.   Received training at the Univ. of Southern California (U.S.C. in 1954 B.Arch).
2.   Practiced some 10 years:
     a.   Apprenticed 2 years as draftsman
     b.   Got California licence in 1957 (age 26)
     c.   Became Associate Architect in 1958 — practice consists of mainly schools and churches.
     d.   Have done all phases of architecture (through drafting, design, working drawings, supervision, client contact, etc.).
     e.   Married an architect — have one child, age 9.
     f.   Presently (for last 7 years) teaching at Los Angeles Trade–Technical College: subjects: drafting (Type V through Type I Construction; Mech. & Elec. Equip for buildings; History of Architecture; Math — Basic through Algebra & Geometry; Materials and Methods of Arch.; and Construction) as an Associate Professor.
     g.   Side note: my twin sister, also is a licensed architect and is currently practicing as P.A. on 3 hospital projects in the greater Los Angeles area.
3.   Re: promotions and discrimination — No. In other areas — yes. In school, at first until sincerity proven; salary — yes. I believe perhaps minmum of 50¢ an hour less. On-job supervision — yes, until proven. I'm not sure, however, that men did not encounter the same (or similar) "having to prove" phenomenon; entirely on another level, perhaps. After this initial period, I feel I have been treated fairly and professionally. Naturally I must *always* use my "titles" when approaching prospective clients or offices or other architects and particularly secretaries, who seem to be the greatest "snobs" of all.

Presently, my goal is to obtain a Ph.D. (or Ed.H.) in Education. I have found teaching more fruitful both monetarily & professionally. Although I do practice during the summers. (By the way, the most difficult client is the friend — I'd starve if I had to live on that business). I feel that architecture is an underrated profession (almost a quasi-profession). In our state we have licensed "Building Engineers"; engineers sign drawings (unethical, in my opinion) and the small [architectural] office has littlel chance — in other words, the public doesn't appreciate professionalism, ethics, and construction quality — so the architect is not respected for these qualities. I feel the architect himself is largely to blame — male *or* female. (By the way, I have seldom thought of myself as a woman architect — simply an architect). I don't appreciate the "quick-and-the-dead" philosophy in any field. (Incidentally there is more discrimination in Education than in the other professions — far more).

What factors led to architecture? I really don't know — its breadth and scope — the artistic combined with the technical — a desire to contribute to the world beyond the scope of the family (which I do not denigrate — parents who were willing to appreciate our dream and support us in our aims, even though I am sure they wondered themselves.

A major factor in my mind was that there were 2 of us — to have undertaken such a task alone, without support during the "low" spots would have been *much* more difficult. Of course, 2 heads are better then one. We joined a social sorority together and I would say had a thoroughly rewarding tenure at the university — intellectually & socially.

LETTER NO. 37
July 1972
West

Your call for help in your research struck a very respon-
sive note here — I am more than willing to help and will write
at length presently. Your letter reached me, however, at a very
difficult time, as I am up to the ears in work: a job just going
out to bid, another with the contractor building the job only two
nails behind what I've drawn, etc. (yes, I am practicing my profession!) and so cannot possibly spare more than a few minutes
to write this note. A couple of weeks, I think, will see me past the
worst of this, and I'll write.

LETTER NO. 38
July 12, 1972
West

I graduated from Univ. of Calif. Berkeley in 1944 with a Bachelor of Arts degree in Architectural Engineering. I was also married in 1944 and now have 4 children ages 26, 24, 17 and 14. I have worked part-time mostly for one Architect and have a very limited practice of my own — mostly residential. In 1967 I became a licensed Building Designer in Calif. In June 1972, I took the complete exam for my Architect's license in Calif. but have not received the results yet. I do intend to continue to take the exam until I pass everything. My children are old enough now so that I can devote more time and energy to the practice of Architecture and I've found that a Building Designer's license is inadequate — I am constantly apologizing and explaining what it means.

I became interested in Architecture initially because it was the logical combination of my two favorite subjects — Art and Math. And the further I got into the subject, the more convinced I became that this was my field.

I have worked in my field ever since finishing college, mostly on a part time basis. I also started my own practice soon after graduation. Raising my family has been my primary occupation but I have always found some time to devote to Architecture. I do thoroughly enjoy my work and an understanding and cooperative husband has been essential. The architect I have worked with for the past 20 years has a very small office so I have been in on almost all phases of the profession. On the job supervision has been limited to my own practice, however, I've held that at a minimum.

Yes, I've found quite a lot of discrimination — not in employment situations but in my independent practice. Clients tend to expect a "better deal" because after all, I'm only a woman. Also, the building trades are impossible — I've been told too often to go back to the kitchen where I belong. Consequently I've done very little supervising on the job. Contractors as a whole, I've found to be fairly decent but prefer that I would just answer questions.

I plan to remain in residential Architecture with my own practice because I do think a woman has an advantage in this area, particularly if she has had experience in keeping house and raising a family. She should have a little better insight concerning how a house should work — it's an ideal situation for a woman.

LETTER NO. 39
February 1, 1972
East

I have not, to any extent, practiced my profession. I graduated from Cornell in 1906 (with two 2ⁿᵈ medals to my credit) took an extra semester on account of illness, specializing in house planning.

My father was Dean of Engineering of Purdue and my first job was a house for him. I did the plans and working drawings (for practice) and supervised the construction, to the disgust of the boss carpenter.

At that time I was married — there was then one architect in the small college town. He was a nice young man and it didn't seem fair to crowd in. I worked with a fellow architect at planning our own house but let him do the drawings. The same arrangement continued for the second house in Washington — where we still live.

Lately some one sent me clippings — comments by women architects in four different countries. They all agreed that being an architect and being a housewife was next to impossible. I am sure I would have found it so.

As a girl I loved drawings — and mathematics — they seemed to point to architecture and my decision never wavered. I was one of a class nine at Cornell — I have of course regretted giving up the career but my happy married life has more than made up for it. I should like to have planned some more houses, since our present one has been much admired. I have enjoyed giving advice to friends who are building — "Face house west if possible" — locate 2ⁿᵈ floor windows above 1ˢᵗ floor — etc., etc.. But when it came to the woman who wanted *all* of the bedrooms to face *southwest*, I gave up.

LETTER NO. 40
1972
Midwest

I became interested in Architecture before I was aware of the term Architecture. Helping my brother maintain a family- owned commercial building at an early age — 12 — gave me an awareness of construction and maintenance and their interdependence.

Lawrence College, Appleton, Wisconsin is where I majored in Math and took an excellent course in Architecture history and a rather weak house design course. That was after 1 year at the University of Michigan Architecture School. The following year I worked in a paper mill and spent four months in Europe. I attended a few architecture classes with a German student in Stuttgart. Upon returning home I thought it was vital to get some experience in an office, but I was terrified to even try. By volunteering to be of "service" just to be able to be in the office — I was taken up on my offer and was thrilled to be in the atmosphere of architecture at work. Eventually I was paid for tracing furniture layouts for an insurance building 2 to 3 weeks, by the hour. In the Fall of 1952, I returned to the University of Michigan for another 11/2 years of training, working summers in some office. My ability to sub for secretary and help type specs was an added attraction I'm sure.

I worked full time and became registered, but did little if any design, mostly detailing and working out others' general design concepts. My first independent project — after design was verbally arrived at in a group — all working drawings was a house Project. Later I became involved in commercial building remodeling: college dormitories, science buildings, manufacturing areas — working drawings and some supervision.

I have experienced more discrimination from below in a position than from above, and was completely unaware of resentment from a few colleagues. Generally there was a fine relationship although there were some patronizing attitudes from some colleagues and contractors who had a little trouble facing the reality of a woman in the field.

Married in 1964 and have not worked in the field since — and don't expect to with 3 children to raise, and a farm.

LETTER NO. 41
March 13, 1972
East

After leaving M.I.T. I was ill for several years so did not pursue architecture. I was advised that unless a woman was wealthy or had relatives in the profession there was little chance for her in that field other than simply becoming a draftsman.

So, eventually I attended Boston Teachers College and went into teaching. I taught mathematics and science in one of the Boston high schools until I retired.

I have had many hobbies. Among them designing and making silver jewelry.

At the present time and for many years my sister (who was also a teacher) and I collected antique dolls and have made about 200 dolls to represent the peddlers of England and Early America.

Together we have written three books on the peddler dolls. We are now writing a fourth book about them.

We are also making and furnishing a doll-house like the old Camp Ground houses of the 1870s found on Martha's Vineyard, Mass. They are sometimes called The American Gothic.

So, during the years, I have kept busy and interested.

LETTER NO. 42
February 2, 1972
East

    Yes I did receive a degree from M.I.T. — but I did not practice; I was married to an engineer soon after and moved as his construction jobs sent us — from Maine to Georgia. We had 5 children and a happy life — ending up back at M.I.T.

    But no architecture. In 1913 no women were accepted in offices and I was offered teaching jobs only. There were women architects before me: Howe and Almy was one office — successful, but no room for more. There have been splendid ones since whose names you must have from the office.

    I never regretted taking the course. It gave me a great interest on the side as we moved around.

LETTER NO. 43
1972
West

I did not start out to be an architect. I had always wanted to be a doctor, and my original study was pre-med. However, as a victim of discrimination, I was transferred to business college, while my brother was kept at the university, when we could not afford for both to stay on at U.C.L.A. I worked in an insurance office until 1941 when free education was offered through the defense training program prior to WW II.

I am telling you this because it serves as an example of the type of discrimination I have faced all of my life. My brother and I are of approximately the same intelligence and ability and have about the same amount of education and experience, yet he has progressed at a much faster rate in his profession than I have. So have my classmates at U.S.C. (all male). Most of them are partners or principals in architectural firms.

The discrimination I have encountered in architecture has mostly been in assignments. It was very difficult at first for me to get on the board. Employers leaned heavily on my business background, and offered me jobs in the contracts, specifications, and brochure departments. When I finally managed to get a comprehensive background in all phases of working drawings, production, and administration, I was usually given the small project in the office, while men with less experience and education got the schools and hospitals.

One of my main reasons for wanting to work at Gruen Associates was that my boss would be not only female but black. She is Director of Architecture and Department Head of Architectural Production. I like my job here, and find little, if any, discrimination in this office on the basis of sex, race, national origin, creed, politics, or anything else. The raises have been slow, but this is true for the men in my job too. As for my goals in architecture, I am contented to be a job captain and deliver a competent set of working drawings consistent with the design concept.

Doris Cole and Sergio Berizzi: Private Residence, Concord, Massachusetts, 1972.
photo: © Steve Rosenthal Photographer.

Doris Cole, principal at Cole and Goyette, Architects and Planners Inc.: Damson & Greengage Restaurant, Boston, Massachusetts, 1987.
photo: courtesy, William T. Smith, Photographer.

Doris Cole, principal at Cole and Goyette, Architects and Planners Inc.: Pennell
Cottage Addition, Shapleigh, Maine, 1994.
photo: courtesy, Nick Wheeler, Photographer.

Doris Cole, principal and Cole and Goyette, Architects and Plnners Inc.: East Boston High School Addition and Renovation, Boston, Massachusetts, 2001. photo: courtesy, Nick Wheeler, Photographer.

Linda Searl, principal at Searl & Associates Inc.; project team, Debra McQueen; Valerio Dewalt Train, Design and Theater Consultants: Oriental Theater Remodeling, Milwaukee, Wisconsin, 1988. photo: courtesy, L. Searl.

Linda Searl, principal at Searl & Associates Inc.; Nancy Willert, Interior Design
Consultant; EagleRiver Financial Corporate Offices, Chicago, Illinois, 1997.
photo: courtesy, © Bruce VanInwegen Photography, L. Searl.

Linda Searl, principal at Searl & Associates Inc.; project team, Amy Graves, Ann Blossfeld, Nancy Willert, Christina Gaswick: Cowell Estate, Grand Traverse Bay, Michigan, 1999. photo: courtesy, © Bruce VanInwegen Photography, L. Searl.

LETTER NO. 44
December 8, 2004
South

I was at a dinner party the other night, and someone asked me the question: Why are there so few women architects in upper management in the big firms? The quick answer to this question is that it's so darn HARD. But it made me stop and think, and in the process, I gathered a few facts.

Our universities are full of women. The undergraduate architectural program at Rice is 60% women and at the University of Houston 55%. But it's downhill from there. Looking at our A.I.A. Houston chapter membership figures, the percentage of women under the age of 30 is only 30%. And in the 30 to 40 age bracket this percentage drops to 20%. Want more bad news? Over age 50 it drops to less than 1%.

Why are women dropping out of our profession? In my opinion, the simple answer is children. The critical career climbing period of our profession is between the ages 25 to 35. These are the years we transition from internship to registration to advancement in a firm. These are also the years women have babies. We have to face the fact that while men are certainly taking on more and more child raising duties, women bear the brunt of the responsibilities. Our society has not advanced to the point where stay-at-home-dads are received with as much admiration from our peers as stay-at-home-moms. When women architects choose to take time off to raise babies, it is often very difficult for them to get back on track when they return. And if the economy is down, the return is even harder.

Most firms are putting out gallant efforts to keep their new mothers working by making them feel as comfortable as possible in the work place. For example, Watkins Hamilton Ross has an in-house Lactating Lounge for nursing mothers complete with refrigerator, comfortable seating and personal lockers. Rey de la Reza Architects keeps a toy chest in their lobby for visiting toddlers. Many firms offer flex time to accommodate mothers who must stay home with sick children. And when the day care center springs an unexpected "In Service Day," children are accepted in the office. I know many mothers who have tried to stay at home with babies and work remotely for the office at the same time, but only in rare cases have I seen this work. The fact is, raising a baby is an all consuming, full-time job.

I like to think that the situation is turning around. We are seeing more and more women in mid-management levels, and they are aggressively moving up. The quality of day care is rising (as is the cost, unfortunately). We now have more mentors in place for those women graduating from our universities, and there are more examples of success stories in how to balance off-spring with the office. But the fact remains, it is HARD work.

AIA National recognizes this. And the problem of under-representation does not lie with women alone. The figures for African Americans, Asians and Hispanics are even fewer. Two years ago, AIA national completed a branding survey which identified the stereotypical image of an architect as that of an able-bodied, straight white male, or the father figure in "The Brady Bunch". The reaction to this was strong, and the 2003 Strategic Plan identified Diversity as one of the most important issues to address. Conferences have been held, committees have formed and the issue is on the front burner among our leaders. Our recently elected AIA National President-Elect is female - Kate Schwennsen, FAIA from Iowa. And hopefully, the trend to hold our national convention on Mother's Day is a thing of the past.

So why is Diversity so important in our profession? As stated by author Kathryn H. Anthony, "The built environment reflects our culture, and vice-versa. If our buildings, spaces, and places continue to be designed by a relatively homogenous group of people, what message does that send about our culture?" Our culture in Houston is diversely rich, and our professional make-up should be the same.

LETTER NO. 45
December 18, 2004
Mid-West

I wanted to be an architect from the time I was 8 years old in 1960. It never occurred to me that women could not be architects. In fact, my best friend's mother was an architect. But when I took a developmental test in 7th grade and the results came back high in mathematics and spatial reasoning, the response was "boys who score high in these areas should become architects, girls should become dress designers." I tried to enroll in shop classes but was firmly told I must take home economics.

While I began college studying Physical Education, I finally switched into Architecture. The teachers at my school were not as bad as those at other schools, who in the 1970s made a point of being tough on women in Architecture. The guise was that they would encounter opposition in the field, and should discover while still in school if they could take it. I had one professor who gave me a B while my other two male team members got A. His response, "You are just going to get married and have kids, you don't need the grade." When I objected, he suggested we play a game of racquetball, his favorite sport. It was determined a game of "cut throat" with the teacher, one of my team mates, and myself would be the best format. I only had to beat one of them to get the A. (Oh, the other qualification was being able to chug a beer!) Little did he know that while racquetball was a relatively new sport on campus, I was the number two women's seed. I chose not to beat the teacher, (bad form) but handily beat the team mate. I received an A after chugging a beer.

Once I graduated I worked for a chauvinistic large firm. The first day on the job, they took several new employees out to a job site. I was required back then to wear a dress or skirt. We visited the job site at lunch time and they made us climb out a third-floor window, and walk across a steel beamed structure with the iron workers eating lunch below. To hoots and howls I had the choice of backing out or walking. I walked.

At Christmas time, it was a tradition for all the ladies to

go up and sit on the owner's lap to get their present . . . a box of nylons (not pantyhose). Once I took the Architectural exam and passed, I refused to do this. I was nearly the only female professional at the firm. My boss came and told me that I had to do it, that it would reflect badly on me if I did not go up to sit on the owner's lap. This was before sexual harassment cases had come to litigation. I told him that not only would I not go, but I demanded the same cash bonus that the men got. This was all the buzz in the office. No one had ever challenged them this way. It was a bad market to get a different job and I wondered if I would survive this. Three months later, I got the bonus, and kept my job.

After I got married I worked for two large firms. At the first I helped design a hospital for children. It took two and a half years, and was so much fun. I loved getting to know the nurses and doctors and seeing the kids get better and move on. Several men before me had been given the task of designing the new neonatal center. None of them had thought to ask the nurses what would make it better, and design after design was shot down. In desperation, they gave it to me. I had the firm send me to the NeoNatal Convention in Georgia, and then spent time talking to the nurses and the parents of the patients. As a result I designed an innovative unit that was replicated around the country. We were the first to build a step down unit, where parents stayed with their preemies for two nights. When buzzers went off on equipment and the baby stopped breathing, they had to call the staff on a phone even though they were just five feet away. It helped the new parents through the difficult stress of taking a preemie home from the hospital. In addition, I worked with the nurses to design a head wall system specifically for premees. It was so rewarding to be able to use architecture to solve problems and make peoples lives better. We talked to the parents of sick children, and discovered them sleeping under their kids' hospital beds. While it is commonplace now, we put in a fold- out chair-bed in each room in addition to a twin sized bed window seat. People were amazed at the things we thought of, but it just came about from LISTENING to the people who were going to use the building.

One of the men I worked with at that firm began a new

area of practice . . . facility programming in the early 1980s, and I worked with him. Subsequently, he moved to another firm and headed the new department. I went with him, and worked part time as I had my children over the next few years. One project went to bid just as I had my second child. The other men on my team moved to other firms, and so when the bid came in too high and we needed to take considerable square footage from the building, I was the only one who knew the project well enough to help. The firm was very good about working around my "new mom" schedule. What a difference ten years had made.

Another client was an insurance company. The firm had designed a wonderful new addition. They asked me to design all of the work spaces and write a program that would allow them to use two different types of interior partitioning systems. After talking to the employees, I came up with the designs for offices, conference rooms, and required support spaces. Then I layed them out in the old building, only to discover that they could fit everything they needed into the existing building with room to spare! They didn't need the new building after all. Leave it to a woman to figure out how to make the space fit. The company was able to postpone the addition for a couple of years.

After my third child, I decided to stay home and just be a mom. I have enjoyed doing set design for the kid's school plays. Some have been very elaborate, with lighted chandeliers and moving sets. In addition, I have enjoyed designing incredible birthday parties for my kids, and Halloween costumes. Can you believe it, I have come full circle. I am designing clothes!

Now that my kids are grown I have started my own practice working in high-end residential (new, renovation, and additions). I am most proud of an 1895 train depot turned into a residence, which received a Homer Award. My dream of being an architect has been fulfilled. What was once thought to be a man's profession has now been opened up to women. And I am proud to be a part of it.

LETTER NO. 46
December 15, 2004
Midwest

When I read the list of questions that you were interested in for your research, I realized that they were questions that I needed to answer for myself. So I will share my answers with you.

I am now 56 years old. I love my life — my husband and I will celebrate our first wedding anniversary this Christmas. He has known me for 11 years and is jealous that I am so content. He needs a job change, too!

My chosen profession is professional harpist. When I was in my 20s and 30s, I was an at-home mom with two children. I taught music in my home and played harp at a restaurant at night.

I loved going to school, so I went to the Community College (it was cheaper) to try computer programming and AutoCad (version 4). Then my husband's aunt left me an annuity, and I decided to go back to school for a Master's degree. In what? That was the question! I knew I needed to be in design (my first degree was anthropology and music), but architecture seemed too scary, so I started in on a Master's in Commercial Interiors. Half way through the program, I was realizing that the graduates were doing facilities management — NOT for me! I dropped out.

When my husband and I divorced, I found it necessary to find a job with a more steady income and the benefits (insurance, 401k). Did it really make any sense to be licensed at 45? Could I pass that test? I talked to the head of the Architecture Department at University of Colorado at Denver. Wow! I could do a 3- year program, the annuity was enough to pay for it, it was 30 minutes from home and credits from the Commercial Interiors program would count. (I was to find out later that more than 1 year would count!)

I was savvy enough to take Auto Cad courses, which got me my first job, right out of college. I was also lucky that it was Denver's high time for architecture jobs.

After the first 3-month job, I moved to a firm that I stayed with for 10 years. The owner was a structural engineer. He was totally unbiased in regard to what women could do (thanks to his mother and wife, who are both personalities), however I know my salary was less because I was not supporting 4 kids. I was even allowed to do the construction administration on a Volkswagen dealership. I made my supervisors aware that I would do any project, but my goal was to be able to take projects from beginning to end. The last project was a 22,000-square foot office condominium that I designed, did CD's and the city review.

I was laid off with no severance and 45 minutes notice when the firm ran into lack of work in the recent slowdown. However, I had the experience (and that last client), and unemployment benefits plus the moral support from my husband to allow me to weather the first year on my own. By the way, this was the same man who pushed me to take the ARE at my first chance — I passed all but one section the first time.

The main thing I missed when I was working 40 hours a week was the harp. I have to say that the first thing I did when I was laid off was to start practicing the harp again and do some heavy soliciting for gigs. Now 1/4 or more of my income comes from the harp.

Now that I am in private practice, home-based, my goal is: make enough money to allow me to stay out of an office. The benefits are:

No commute allows me time to exercise instead.

No time clock allows me to teach some students in the daytime, practice 1 to 2 hours in the middle of the day, and perform in the daytime.

I plan to continue beyond retirement age, at whatever hours I please.

I keep an open mind on jobs. Since I did several car dealerships and offices, I feel comfortable with small commercial projects. I am just starting on a warehouse/office and tenant finish for the office condominium (yes, that client was excited when I was laid off!). I have also been doing residential additions and basement finish. I enjoy commercial jobs and the city interaction (6 different municipalities so far in the Denver metropolitan area). My other true love is Historic Preservation. I live in a 101 year-old house. My fun project this past year was the exterior elevations, details, and some cabinetry and kitchen design for a new Victorian house to be built in the mountains.

LETTER NO. 47
December 14, 2004
South

What factors in your life led you to architecture?
My father is an architect, so I grew up with this profession — and I love cities.

Where did you receive your professional training?
M. Arch, M.I.T.

What types of projects and what phases (design, working drawings, supervision, etc.) of the projects have you done?

As Owner and Principal of my professional practice, I do all phases of most projects. During the years I worked for others, I was primarily a designer. My professional work is increasingly interdisciplinary and includes collaboration with a colleague in landscape architecture. As tenured member of an architecture school faculty, my work includes teaching, writing, lecturing — and mentoring others beginning in the profession.

Have you been subjected to discrimination in salary, job promotions, etc. due to your sex?

Sadly, yes — although not in the academic world. In the world of professional practice, the difficulty has been one of equitable access to a range of projects.

What are some of your goals in architecture?

Design, Build, Write, Teach — in order to shape a better world.

LETTER NO. 48
December 29, 2004
Midwest

What factors in your life led you to Architecture?
I knew I was capable to carry a profession beyond the typical professions/jobs associated with women. And, I was interested in Architecture since I am a native of Greece.

Where did you receive your professional training?
I started in Greece (3 years), and received my Bachelors in Architecture from the University of Illinois in Chicago, and Masters in Architecture from the University of Illinois in Urbana/Champaign. I worked in Greece at Doxiadis' office, and Chicago's Department of Public Works at the City Architect's office.

Have you practiced your profession?
Yes, upon my licensing I opened my office, we just celebrated our 25th year.

What types of projects /phases have you done?
Mostly public projects.

Have you been subjected to discrimination in salary, job promotions etc?
I have not spent enough time in an architectural corporate setting, so I do not have a lot to say about that. Being entrepreneurial, I moved on without paying much attention to that. Although I knew that men were looked upon with more serious possibilities.

What are some of your goals in Architecture?
With a few legacy projects under our belt so far, I hope it continues.

On personal reflections, while most of my women classmates have their own offices, I don't see the younger generation of women architects opening their own offices. That is surprising.

LETTER NO. 49
January 3, 2005
South

What factors in your life led you to architecture?
As a child, I was drawing house plans on graph paper, so at
the very least, I was into space planning. I also enjoyed art
class: sculpture, painting, drawing; and I enjoyed (and was
good at) math. So I guess the basic ingredients were there for
architecture.

I was offered a scholarship in engineering, which I would
appreciate a lot more now, but at the time it seemed it would be
too much math, that design would be dictated by math and not
much else. I wish I had known more about it then.

I got an undergraduate degree in cultural history, which
included some classes in architectural history and the history of
cities. I went to France the summer after my sophomore year,
and Israel the next summer, and the most fascinating things to
me were the buildings. In Israel I was looking at very modern
(contemporary) architecture (in Tel Aviv) and I realized that if
even the modern stuff fascinated me — since as a history major,
I thought that mostly the "old" stuff would keep my attention
— maybe that's what I wanted to do. It's as close to having a call-
ing as I will probably ever get. So I went back to school for my
senior year, and my advisor told me about programs for a 3-year
master's degree in architecture, which is what I did.

Where did you receive your professional training?
My undergraduate degree (B.A.) is from the University of
Wisconsin (Madison). My master's degree in architecture is
from the University of Wisconsin-Milwaukee.

*Have you practiced your profession? If you have not prac-
ticed architecture, what were some of the reasons?*
I practiced in the very traditional sense for the first 10 years
of my career. I worked in small architectural practices (2 to 20
people). Since I didn't ever design a complete building, I'm not
sure if my experience really could be considered "practicing."
I've gotten to choose/design components to buildings, and
I've worked with older architects discussing design aspects of

buildings, but I never designed a building myself.

After 10 years, I was somewhat bored and/or burnt out, so I switched to working at a seaport in Florida in the construction management division. I stopped doing traditional practice, and went into project management. This suited me better at that time, because I got more involved with construction which I really enjoy, and since I was at a port, some of the projects were more aligned with engineering than architecture, so the work was varied. The other aspect of project management that I appreciate is that it is generally better paid than architecture.

What types of projects and what phases (design, working drawings, supervision, etc.) of the projects have you done?
I have done commercial projects: office buildings, banks, schools, hotels, tenant spaces in malls, model homes, and libraries. I have done governmental projects for ports and airports: passenger terminals, warehouses, garages, tenant spaces, space planning (cubicles), fire stations, crane maintenance facility, emergency operation centers, and a cargo entry gate. I was involved with a small portion of design (components but not the overall look), and also working drawings, supervision of consultants on some, computer work, planning, research, programming, bidding, and construction.

Have you been subjected to discrimination in salary, job promotions, etc. due to your sex?
In the Port industry there is definitely a glass ceiling. Since the port I worked at was part of a county government system, I could advance up to a point, but I knew I would have a very hard time becoming an assistant director, let alone director. In some of the other port divisions (i.e. business or finance) there were female directors, but I think it would be hard to do that in the construction division.

What are some of your goals in architecture?
I don't think of myself as a typical architect. I lean much more to the technical/construction side of the business than the design side. That said, I would like to go into the construction industry, maybe as a project manager. I just love seeing the process of constructing a building.

However, after going to my first (and last, I believe) A.I.A. state convention this past August, I have started to think more about design. It's almost like going back to my roots. So I am also considering how to get involved more with the design side of the industry as well.

LETTER NO. 50
January 3, 2005
West

I recently sat on a panel discussion for the University of Colorado, "Women in Architecture." The highly accomplished panelists spanned five decades; I represented the youngest amongst the panelists, at 36 (graduating from Carnegie Mellon in 1989). The challenges discussed were great, juggling a highly engaging and intensive profession in a primarily male profession, with the obligations of family. The obligations of a family were pressing for the women represented, who often felt the need to be the primary care-givers for children, care for a spouse, run a household, care for aging parents as well as break into a male dominated profession. More interesting than the personal challenges each women faced in the profession, however was the large and engaged male portion of the audience who merely wanted to glean information from each of the highly accomplished women.

My generation is the turning point for female architects. My career has spanned the distance in the profession where I confronted my first interview at 23 with the questions about my marital status and desire to have children "architecture is much too demanding for a family," paid 75% the salary of my male peers (with the same education and experience), and greeted with a cat-call and whistle when first walking onto a job site as a project architect. Today, I am still greeted with skepticism, a "young" female architect (my physical appearance is about 6 years younger than my age). As project architect, when entering a job site trailer with a junior male architect, questions first turn to the male architect. I overcome these misconceptions in the way I responded to a very petite woman at the University of Colorado lecture who asked "how do you gain respect on a construction site when, unlike many of my male peers I have never lifted a hammer?" easy, was my response, "you just need to be the smartest and most prepared person in the room, people will turn to you for answers".

Women, and the stereotype of their ability to "multitask," and collaborate make females adept for the challenges of a changing profession. Clients, stakeholders, and project demands are becoming more complex, and the construction industry is changing, as women are becoming superintendents and project managers for contractors.

As with our male counter-parts the rewards of a creative profession are worth the challenge, commitment and sacrifice. The most rewarding moments of my life have been walking in a building conceived of in my mind.

LETTER NO. 51
January 4, 2005
Northwest

I have been continuously employed in the practice of architecture since matriculating with my Master of Architecture degree from the University of Illinois in 1977 (B. Arch. Studies from U. of Illinois in 1975). I actually began working during the summers in a local A/E office while in high school, as an architectural draftsperson — using experience gained in my high school architectural drawing classes in Champaign, Illinois. I continued with summer drafting work with the same A/E firm as it was available during my undergraduate years, since the real life experience in practice was valuable to me. When it was not available, I drafted materials rupture graphs for graduate students at the U of Illinois Engineering Department of Testing and Materials — watching concrete cylinders explode was fun! While working towards my M. Arch., I spent summers doing coursework, since I was employed as an Architectural Design Teaching Assistant in the U. of Illinois School of Architecture with 20 contact hours per semester teaching sophomore and junior architectural design studios.

You asked what led me into the profession. I decided on architecture in the 6th grade after briefly considering becoming an astronaut (but reconsidered because I was extremely nearsighted and couldn't become a pilot — it did not occur to me then that I would probably not make the cut due to my gender). Probably it was my maternal grandmother who influenced me the most- — she raised me. Grandma would take me on walking tours around our Midwestern city, stopping to critique buildings and their design elements — especially the construction details. She had been married to a general contractor, who finally gave her her own set of hand tools so she would stop borrowing his. I believe that, given a different set of circumstances, she might have entered the profession herself. Grandma had been born in 1896 on a quarter-homestead farm near the Illinois river. Though winning a scholarship to the land-grant college that became the University of Illinois, her father told Grandma that she could not attend, since he could not afford to also send his 2 sons to college. Though Grandma was not a bra-burner, she nevertheless became an ardent feminist, and she convinced me that I could become anything I damned well wanted to! I was careful not to let her down — I also won a full academic scholarship to attend the U of Illinois beginning in 1971.

It certainly sounds like you are familiar with the 1970s from your own experiences. The recession in those years was devastating to our profession: I have weathered two more since, but neither of these seemed as difficult as the mid to late 70s. The major reason I accepted the T.A. position and stayed in school from 1975 to 1977 was that none of the architectural firms I wanted to work with were capable of hiring: they were kind in interviewing me, and were encouraging regarding my portfolio, but had had to lay off many of their own staff during those years. So, I gratefully accepted the teaching position and stayed in school 2 more years, even though I was itching to practice. Actually, teaching the four consecutive sophomore and junior design classes helped me to consolidate my own design theory, and was an experience I now would not trade for the best entry-level position with a big-name architectural firm.

I had always thought I would end up practicing in Chicago (so many of our Illinois graduates do) but the jobs seemed to become available earlier in the St. Louis area. I accepted an entry position in August 1977 in a firm of approximately 20 persons, and sat for my Missouri Board exam in 1980. Early projects as a P.A. were a K-12 school, speculative office buildings (from modern custom curtainwall to more traditional load-bearing masonry buildings). I would highly recommend starting out working in small firms, where it is possible to follow projects from programming through construction as I did. This was a great foundation for me, especially working first-hand code with officials, consultants and contractors early in my professional years. I still cherish memories of the people (all male, actually) who mentored and befriended me during that time. A small firm allows people to belong, and feel centered. I still keep in contact with a few of my drafting-room contemporaries from those days, exchanging mail at least once a year.

I met my husband (now of 28 years) soon after beginning

to practice. Probably it will be of no surprise to you that he is also an architect! I have since observed many more matches in our profession (perhaps we work so many hours that we don't get out much — but I prefer to think that architects are basically just basically good people). My husband and I travel well together, since we both want to poke about in the new and historic buildings wherever we may go. I suppose we get on well because I'm more focused on client relationships, programming, and design, while my husband loves design development, the construction process, and QA/QC. This makes us a "firm in a box" — more about that later!

As a newly licensed architect, I had the ambition to move on to a larger firm of 125, in St. Louis. Not coincidentally, my husband had recently accepted a position with them, and I had grown to know the partners socially. They are still in business, and a fine group, probably best known for their relationship with Anheuser Busch (architects for the corporate HQ, Busch Gardens, Sea Worlds, etc.). There were a handful of female interns, younger than me, at that time. One was working with my husband, and she so appreciated his mentoring in the basics that we still receive Christmas cards from her. I was working as a team architect on the design development of the NORAD Space Command at Peterson A.F.B., Colorado, when the firm had the opportunity to work on a 33-acre Masterplan for Hunt Oil's development firm in Dallas, Texas. They asked my husband and me to open their branch office and form the core team for this exciting project. We agreed, and they moved us to Dallas in 1981. We hired a staff of about 15 to perform work for this client and a few others. It was an exciting time for large-scale architectural development throughout the southern half of the country, so when they wished to close the branch in 1983 following conclusion of the Masterplan project, we elected to stay in Dallas for a while, and chose to work with different, established regional firms. I went to a 35-year-old practice with 100 or so people. I encountered a senior female architect for the first time — she had been with the firm from their early days, and retired from practice while I was there. We had a number of female Interior Designers as well.

I stayed with them for 13 years until 1996. From Project

Architect I became a Project Manager and a minor stockholder in the firm. My proudest accomplishments to date are from these years: a one-million s.f. highrise office building leased as the headquarters for First Union National Bank (now Wachovia) in downtown Charlotte, N.C., plus a 500,000 s.f. shell and core office building for the same developer (Childress Klein Properties) in Atlanta's N.E. perimeter area. RJR Nabisco leased the entire Atlanta building as their headquarters, though it was built "on spec." As a Project Manager, I became frustrated that the male building designers would not "step inside the front door" to design the multi-story building lobbies and public spaces — frustrating me because I needed to coordinate the building core and positions for escalators, tenant storefronts and the like. I solved my own staffing issue by designing the core and lobby spaces down to the custom building entrances, door pulls, lighting fixtures, and furniture. This opened other opportunities for the design of the exterior public plazas, fountains and the ground floor customer spaces such as the flagship bank and investment center for First Union. I suppose you could call this "Interior Architecture." Interestingly, the male design architects would not "trust" the firm's interior designers to perform any portion of this work (and largely, these folks were not qualified to do it, sadly! The interior designers at that firm for the most part picked colors and furniture). The spaces I designed were well received by the public and tenants, and the work led me to serve First Union for many more "inside-outside" design projects. We re-built three out of four street corners at College and Third Streets in downtown Charlotte together: the plazas and fountains "talk" to one another across the streets, and helped to enliven the downtown core. I still keep in contact with First Union's director of Corporate Architecture, long after I've moved on and this firm has passed out of existence.

Also while at this firm I managed several projects in the design process for some of the Texas public universities, ending up with a new student center built at Texas State Univ.-Corpus Christie the year I chose to leave Texas — 1996. That was fun because it was all about creating people spaces — inside, outside, up and down. It is a joyful building, and an icon for the young campus.

An editorial comment here: there is no concerted coordination effort that I can perceive between the schools of architecture and the schools of interior design to promote mutual respect between our closely related professions. For licensing and market-share reasons, many architects are distrustful of interior designers, and vice versa. For women architects, this can lead to some strange situations: in interviewing with firms I have more than once been approached by male principals who have been desirous of hiring me as an architect, but almost at the last minute suggest that I could also really help them organize their interior designers (I have consistently rejected these job offers, because this singles me out due to my gender). Finally I am working in a very large (470-person) office combining architects, interior designers and graphics and branding professionals — all on a fairly level footing. This is utopia. More importantly, our collaboration serves the needs of our clients, most of whom have both an "inside" and an "outside" to their customers or employees' environments.

After 15 years in Texas, I absolutely could not stand to live there anymore. There is no "there" in Dallas — no real urbanity, and the few pedestrians that brave the sidewalk-less neighborhoods take their lives in their hands. There are some charming towns in Texas, but the climate and salt-water deprivation (my husband and I are sailors and divers) led me to think about locating elsewhere. I also had an inkling that the firm would be sold to a national firm — and, indeed it was taken over 8 short months after we moved to Seattle. I will be forever grateful to my husband for giving up job, friends, and clients and relocating to Seattle due to my mid-life crazies.

We both interviewed in Portland and Seattle. Seattle was an easy choice for both of us (we were able to move our blue-water sailing yacht from an inland Texas lake, after all). Specifically, I had targeted a firm which has succeeded through helping make our clients successful. We provide better environments for our clients' customers, employees, and patients. Corporate clients I have served since at this firm include Microsoft, Boeing (the WHQ move to Chicago) and Washington Mutual Bank (various administrative buildings and data centers). I've been the PM for the S.F. Giants Corporate HQ and retail Dugout store (attached to HOK's lovely ball park), Taubman Company's Bay Street/ Tampa International Plaza projects, numerous malls for Millennium Development (the Seibu Department Store's development arm in Tokyo), including a full city block of neighborhood shopping and restaurant venues eight stories high in Yokohama, Japan. I'm currently managing a large Port of Seattle, Aviation Division project to provide a base for travelers renting cars at the airport — 8000 vehicles in and out per day at peak summer capacity in 2020. The expansive customer-service building is the first airport image one will see upon entering our densely-packed urban airport.

I lead project teams of between 4–15 persons. We are a diverse firm, with women in practically every job description. Every continent and practically every race on earth is represented here, and these cultural sensibilities help us with our approach to the design of our international projects. You asked about my goals. I continue to believe that through architecture we are able to lend dignity to people's everyday lives. I also believe that architects and planners need to work more closely together to create urban environments which mix living, working, and playing in the same physical area — most urban zoning still does not support this (especially in the sun belt states). All projects should be approached as mixed-use projects! That is a goal I am actively able to pursue with our clients — which is why I will likely be staying here until I choose to retire.

Another editorial comment: Japanese architects and contractors are reverential towards American architects — especially senseis who have taught at university level. While traveling to Japan for over a year and a half, I learned to speak Japanese conversationally (believing it is rude not to be able to inquire about our hosts' health, family, etc.). Architects and contractors there work very collaboratively (actually, most architects there work for contracting firms) largely because is little litigation in the building industry. A person's word is still very highly regarded. I wish we could return to these principles in the U.S.!

My husband has retired after 52 years in the profession, with many rewarding projects and associations of his own. I have two step-children (my husband's children by a previous marriage), 4 step-grandchildren, and 1 step-great-grandchild! It has been wonderful seeing the grandkids grow to adulthood. None have chosen to become architects, but are contributing to the world in their own unique ways. I am grateful for the friendship of the children, who are contemporaries of mine.

You asked if I have experienced any discrimination in salary or promotions. The answer is no, I do not believe so. Since 1981, I have been employed in firms large enough that such practices would be considered a federal offense, anyway. More discreetly, I do not believe that I have been mentored as readily as some of my male contemporaries in some — but by no means all — cases. People tend to be most comfortable with others who look just like themselves, right? I have consciously tried to not let this outmoded principle affect me as I endeavor to equally mentor the men and women who work under me. Interestingly, I have found no apparent discrimination on behalf of my clients — actually, I believe some of my First Union work resulted from a female bank V.P. reviewing my proposals and rejoicing in the opportunity to give the work to another woman! This is a small fact that male architects seldom figure out — some continue to see female associates or partners as more of a liability than an asset. Human Resources departments are beginning to be found in some of the larger architectural offices — quite a change for the profession, and good for everyone.

My only regret is that I did not come to Seattle to practice soon after graduation — it is a wonderful city. I believe it still claims the highest per-capita percentage of licensed architects in the country, which says any number of things. Thankfully, there currently seems to be plenty of work to go around. Of course, my journey through the mid-section of this country with my husband was exceptional — and I would not trade that — it helps us both appreciate the quality of life we have achieved here.

Marilys R. Nepomechie, principal at Marilys R. Nepomechie Architects; landscape and graphic design, Marta Canaves; project team, Ricardo Herran, Daniel Romero, Julio Pulido: Scattered Site Infill Housing for Little Haiti, Miami, Florida, 2001. photo: courtesy, M. Nepomechie.

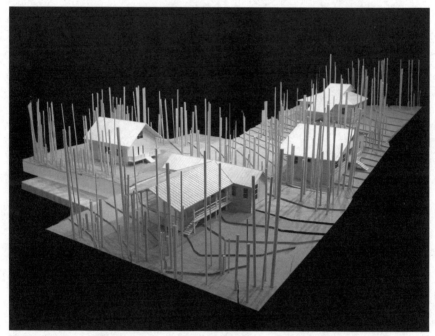

Marilys R. Nepomechie, principal at Marilys R. Nepomechie Architects; landscape
and graphic designer, Marta Canaves; project team, Luis Asturias, Carlo
Giammattei, Marina Giammattei, Michael Figueroa; Affordable Single-family
Housing, Rural Appalachia, Rowan County Eastern Kentucky, 2003.
photo: courtesy, M. Nepomechie.

Marilys R. Nepomechie, architect and Marta Canaves, landscape design, curators / designers; project team, Lester Ray, Charlene West, Marina Giammattei, Carlo Giammattei, Julio Pulido: Miami / La Habana, Mare Nostrum, An Installation / Exhibition, 2nd International Architecture Biennale, Rotterdam, The Netherlands, 2005.
photo: courtesy, M. Nepomechie.

Laurie Smith: The Historic Frisco Train Depot Adaptive Reuse, Kirkwood, Missouri, 2006. photo: courtesy, Agap Construction Company.

LETTER NO. 52
January 14, 2005
South

I recently was sent a copy of an article printed in the *Toronto Globe and Mail* entitled "Female Architects Seen Running For Exits." The text clearly outlined the inequality of the numbers of registered women architects, 31% in Ontario, compared to the equal numbers of each sex entering architecture school and then it went on to list the numbers of women who are actually practicing in the field which is only 13%. This is from a country where the socialistic attitude is easier on the working female especially since the cost of living is so high that both partners in a marriage are usually in the work force. The last figure I got for the U.S. is about 8% of the registered practicing architects are female.

The next item in my mail was a newsletter from my liability insurance company stating that the number of law suits against architects is increasing severely and it is not from professional liability action. The majority of the increase in suits filed against architectural firms are related to sexual harassment and discrimination in the work place. This was a surprise since it means that the same firms who are trying to convince clients that they are the leading edge in design for the work place, don't understand what it takes for the most fair and effective functioning of business.

This is not a career that can be taken lightly considering the long hours, pressure and intimidation, especially on the construction site, but I have found the contractors far easier to deal with than fellow architects or engineers. The contractor often doesn't like the architect to begin with, but the female on a construction site may actually temper this due to her less competitive nature, while she still may have to endure stares and cat calls from the construction laborers. Architects have perpetuated the arrogant "my drawings are perfect" attitude for decades now and this is not very realistic considering that the average young architects copying details by computer, may not even understand the elements they are drafting let alone the actual method of construction. Most architects have never had to physically build a wall or pour a slab in place and thus they have no empathy for the contractor. I was quite fortunate to attend Yale for my graduate degree, where Charles Moore helped set up the first year construction program which made it mandatory for each student to spend at least two weeks of manual labor on a community oriented building project. I have personally gone on to work as a design/build contractor and carpenter so I have never had a problem collaborating with the contractors on my projects and I like to promote the "team" attitude. So the problem for the female architect seems to stem from more from internal forces in the profession.

I remember my first job in an architecture firm during the summer of 1974, when I was sixteen. I was sent down into the ammonia-filled basement to run prints in a space wallpapered with Playboy centerfolds. I was next assigned to clean out the drawers, a job that was created just for me, until they figured out that I could actually draft, quite well too, and I spent the rest of the my summer working on a drafting board located so that the senior project manager could easily peer down my shirt, which he tried often. I went on to eventually work at one of the most prestigious firms in Toronto and during my first week there the senior partner came into the design studio, stood with arms crossed in front then leaned down to stare under the drafting tables and proceeded to rate the legs of the female architects. He then asked the attractive woman next to me what her name was. She told him that it was Stacey and he went on to say that he knew that it had to be something like Tracy, Stacey or Bambi.

These are the more amusing incidents but I have also been a victim of threats, hostility and witnessed blatant avoidance of both hiring and promoting women in the field. Female architects are often put in the interiors department or they become work horses who aren't allowed to meet with the client except as an assistant to a male colleague. One major client in Charlotte actually refused to allow any females to attend meetings for his projects, so a male front man was sent in to take my place even though I was the project architect. In another large firm, an outside marketing company was brought in to assess the firm's ability to go national in a specific field of architecture. After extensive interviews with the staff and review of the practice, a report was generated which red flagged the existing sexual harassment within the firm and potential legal pitfalls of this situation. To their credit, the firm immediately isolated the five main culprits and advised them to participate in sessions to improve their behavior.

Besides the difficulties created by the attitudes of fellow professionals, the female architect faces incredible guilt about having to leave work for a sick child, school activities, doctors appointments, and — maternity leave. Maternity leave alone is enough to scare firms away from hiring a female. They worry about spending time training a worker only to have them decide to not go back to work after having a child and being pregnant in an all-male competitive world is extremely hard especially with the long hours that firms encourage. You do get a sense that you have to work that much harder to make up for these inconveniences. Pay is also a problem with female architects and sometimes we actually hurt ourselves in that respect by not knowing what our other male counterparts are earning or undervaluing ourselves. The assumption is that the male architect may be supporting a family while the female's is a secondary income.

During my pregnancies, I worked up until the delivery day and then I took phone calls regarding projects while I was in the hospital. I requested that my doctor induce my labor for each of my children to ensure my schedule would not be disrupted by a surprise delivery. This was also for my children's best interest because I had extremely short labors and my doctor was concerned that I might be on-site or stuck in traffic when labor began. What do you do though, if you want to breast feed? Do you have to choose between your child or your job? I was fortunate to either have been working at an enlightened firm or my own practice when this question came up for me regarding each of my four children. I was able to bring my babies to the work place and they slept under my desk in a basket then I would breast feed in my own office or a washroom until they were old enough to stay home with a nanny. My children have attended many client meetings and visited job sites from age five days old until they have left home for college. I have been blessed with compassionate and understanding clients as well as some extraordinary employers/partners. I once heard Anita Rodrick, founder of the Body Shop, speak at a function and say that one of her favorite sights was that of a woman in an office at a computer, breast feeding. This concept shocked me at first, until I realized that this was what I had done and it made my life better balanced for my family and I was a much more productive and happy employee.

I understand that it is much easier for a company to avoid all this negotiation for flexible scheduling by avoiding hiring females but this doesn't solve the ongoing problem. The practice can benefit from the input that the women architects can bring to the table. *The Globe and Mail* article pointed out that women make good architects which is proven since they win at least half of the design awards and without them, the field is losing some of it's most talented practitioners. Women are skilled at communication, consensus seeking and multi-tasking which are beneficial in architecture teams and there are more females becoming clients especially in the Health Care field.

These problems that women architects are encountering are ones that the architect profession itself has created especially when the majority of business has recognized that, whether they agree with the program or not, times have changed and the female employee is out there looking for equal treatment and some professional flexibility in order to stay with a firm. Women are a valuable commodity to the business world, they have much to offer and we need to tap into that resource and provide the tools to accommodate their needs to be more productive.

I have encountered many difficulties to overcome since deciding to become an architect when I was just thirteen in the 9th grade. I began my ambition by taking all the architectural and mechanical drafting classes I could in the tech wing of the high school. Of course I was one of the very few girls to even venture into this dark, crude section of the school for vocational training that smelled of oil and grease. When I tried to take an auto mechanics class one term, I was told by the Department. Chairman that "as a female I would be a hazard to myself and my fellow students." I was not allowed to attend that class but I was able to switch into electricity class, which was much more dangerous to me than working on a car, but luckily the Chairman didn't see it that way. I gained a valuable skill in that class that has helped me become a more well- rounded architect.

As I was finishing high school, I applied to Waterloo University in Ontario which had an excellent architecture school, and even though I was accepted into the architecture department, (only 10% of applicants were) I was rejected from the school itself since my high school teachers had gone on strike 3 of my 4 years and I was missing critical English requirements. This was devastating to me since I was determined to be an architect especially after I had spent my summers working at several architecture firms and construction companies which reinforced my love of building design and the construction business. I was forced to reassess an acceptance letter from a relatively small architecture school in the States that I had applied to as a contingency. Miami University had an excellent reputation and I was fortunate to do my undergraduate work for my Bachelor of Environmental Design on that campus. I also continually took summer design studios, one at Cornell as well, and finished my four year degree in three, a feat that had not occurred in the school before. In fact, the Dean would only allow me to finish early if I was accepted into one of the top schools in the country for my graduate degree and luckily, I received an acceptance letter from Yale.

Since finishing my Master's of Architecture in 1982, my working experience as a professional in the field of architecture has spanned everything from hand drawing on velum through to the elaborate computer drafting and rendering programs that are currently being used in the industry. I have been fortunate to have been given guidance early in my career by some dedicated mentors, one project manager in Vancouver and a partner in Toronto as well as more recent assistance from a couple partners of a firm in Charlotte. This career has been a passion and when I go to speak at career day at the local high schools, I do try to be realistic about the difficulties of code requirements, liabilities, extended work hours, the lower pay in this field but temper that with the joy of seeing an idea brought to fruition and a positive contribution made to society. I have taken my knowledge and volunteered to help my community as a Board of Variance member, Planning Commissioner, and lecturer. I have also had the privilege of participating in a large variety of project types from exciting thirty story high-rise buildings and million sq.ft. malls to small personal residential projects.

While I have also worked at various types of firms in both Canada and the United States as an employee or partner, my opinion remains that the best way for a female to truly enjoy the practice of architecture is through self-employment and I have been lucky to have had my own firm for the majority of my thirty-year career in this amazing profession.

LETTER NO. 53
January 20, 2005
Midwest

FACTORS
Various family members are/ were involved in engineering, architecture, and the arts. I have talent in math, science, and the visual arts.

TRAINING
Wellesley, pre-architecture, 1967–9
Stanford, B.A. Architecture + Urban Design, 1972
Princeton, M.A. Architecture, 1975

PRACTICE
Northrup Kaelber + Kopf, Rochester, NY, designer, vacation-time during schooling, 1970–1975
Ehrenkrantz Group, New York, NY, designer, 1975–1977
SOM, Chicago, IL, partner, 1977–1989 (first female partner of SOM; also first female partner to leave voluntarily)
DLK Civic Design, Chicago, IL, owner/ principal, 1989-present (Women Business Enterprise)

PROJECTS
My experience includes virtually all types of projects and all phases from programming and feasibility thru contract documents and construction administration, including municipal, federal, transportation (aviation, transit, highways), infrastructure [streets + bridges], exhibition, mixed use and office (low to high-rise), health care, commercial, recreation (parks, racetrack, stadium, waterfront), museums, newspaper, human services, and corporate. My firm focuses on projects in the public realm: transportation and infrastructure plus civic places+spaces.

DISCRIMINATION
I was "picked on" while the only female student in the engineering department at Stanford. My partners at SOM assumed that I would quit practice once I became pregnant, and began to discount my efforts to balance family + practice (my pay was cut). I finally left SOM just before I delivered my second of three children, because I did not want to travel overseas and I was more interested in civic/ public projects than commercial/ development projects

GOALS

As I wind down my "corporate" life, I will continue to contribute my time and talents to civic organizations (recently completed a three-year tenure on the Mayor's Zoning Reform Commission and am currently assisting a new Chicago charter school develop their curriculum for architecture, engineering, and construction-bound students). I will continue to help citizens make positive changes in their communities — through the design process itself, the design of public space and places, and the development of "civitas" within our communities, large and small.

LETTER NO. 54
January 28, 2005
Midwest

I was born on Chicago's south side, chose to study Architecture after majoring in Biology, then Landscape Architecture. It was while studying the urban landscape of London and spending weeks in the library of the R.I.B.A. that led to a personal revelation to become an architect. I graduated from the University of Illinois at Chicago. Before establishing my own firm, I worked for three prominent Chicago figures in architecture, Harry Weese, Stuart Cohen, and Thomas Beeby, all mentors in my professional development. I have been the Principal of my own firm since 1985 and have completed more than 340 projects, ranging from small residential additions to the remodeling of the Grand Concourse of Soldier Field in Chicago into a memorial to American Veterans. In recent years, my practice has expanded beyond the Midwest and we have completed projects from New York City to Seattle.

Observations:

Cities are built on the common purpose of respecting one's neighbor and this same purpose should hold true to architecture. We must create a graceful, respectful civic architecture, an architecture in concert with its context and prominence. There is a drive for design of a contrarian willfulness that I find most disturbing. There is need for thoughtful buildings that are quiet background to our more prominent civic institutions. The hierarchy of prominence is skewed.

I'm very worried about contemporary architectural education. I have noticed a sharp decline of building science skills, understanding of what a LINE must represent, an unproductive fascination with computer modeling and technology that neither creates a better set of construction documents nor enhances the built form. There is a disconnect between the skill to visualize and draft. They also lack the ability to free-hand draw to scale, which will always be a necessary skill in meetings or on site. The computer has been falsely assigned the ability to create perfection. Young architects don't realize that the computer is only as smart and as "perfect" as the information that is fed into it by our less-than-perfect abilities. I remain optimistic that, as these young architects hone the real necessary skills for design and building, that they will place the computer in its rightful position — next to the other tools for drawing.

I have had twenty wonderful years running my own practice. It certainly is not one without the challenges of the economic swings of most architectural practices, but one with a continuum of great clients and inspiring assignments. I am most grateful for all the opportunities that my clients have entrusted me with. It has often occurred to me that there is a built-in screening device of my clientele, a type of self-selection process has been going on. An individual, a couple, a company who selects a woman-owned business in an industry that is dominated by men, indicates an open-mindedness, a lack of prejudice, and a belief in expanding opportunity. It is not a coincidence that I have clients who have become close friends, returned several times for our services or who remain respected colleagues.

LETTER NO. 55
March 8, 2005
Midwest

The factors that led to my becoming an architect are slightly fuzzy. I didn't really know anyone who was an architect, and I grew up in a small town in Florida. There was a third grade teacher of mine whose husband was an architect, who worked on FLW"s Florida Southern College, but I think my teacher was the influence, since I don't specifically remember meeting her husband.

My mother was probably the greatest influence. She always said you can be whatever you want to be. She was a teacher and somehow got interested in politics and ran for a seat on the city commission. By the time I was in high school (1962–65) she was the mayor, elected by the city council. She was the first woman mayor in Florida of a city over 50,000 people.

I went to a girls' school my first year of college, because I had been discouraged about architecture by friends and teachers. After the first semester, I realized that this was not the school for me, and that I really wanted to try architecture school. My quote here is "architecture school can't be any worse than this."

So I went back to Florida, U. of Florida, in Gainesville and said to myself that I would try architecture for one year to see if I liked it. It was difficult and challenging, but I loved that first year. The second year was more difficult for me, because we started to design buildings, which I really knew nothing about. My teacher for this third year design studio, was fairly young. He suggested to me that women were not really "meant to be architects." I dropped out of design after that year and took all of the technical courses, and then want back to design in my fourth year. So it took six years to do the five-year program, (including my year at the girls' college) but ultimately I did well.

There were two other women in the program at this time, each one year apart. I worked during the summer breaks at an architect's office in Lakeland, and found the work repetitive and not very stimulating. This led to my decision to get a Masters degree, so that I could teach architecture, which I did immediately after graduate school for seven years.

I was concerned that if I entered an office directly out of school I would be given tasks that were not challenging and meaningful, nor would I really learn anything during the experience.

After seven years at two different schools, where I discovered that I was being paid less than my male counterparts with less education and experience than I had, I decided that I couldn't teach anymore without having practiced myself. So I moved to Chicago in 1980.

Teaching was a wonderful experience because it gave me the opportunity to think more clearly about what I really believed about design and the profession. Both of the schools where I taught were new schools, and needed to develop their programs, library, and faculty. The faculty was in general all young and energetic, and we spent our days and nights devoted to these schools

I began working in an office in Chicago. This is also when it became more apparent that there were still not many women in this profession and I was very lonely for more interaction with them. A group called Chicago Women in Architecture was in existence and I joined that organization soon after moving to Chicago. This group was very supportive and nurturing, especially for young women coming into the profession. Over a five-year period in Chicago two women in architecture exhibits were launched by CWA. I worked in an office during this time, learning how to develop a set of drawings and really put a building together. Jack Hartray was one of the partners, and was one of the best mentors for young people in the office. He was, and still is, a great teacher, with patience for any question he is asked.

But I also realized that there would never be an opportunity to become a partner in this firm. Because of some of my associations from CWA I met a woman who was about to start her own firm.

We discussed the idea of a partnership and tried it for a few months before making it official. This partnership lasted five years, but broke up because we both had egos after all and both wanted to be the design partner of the firm.

Our work was primarily residential, based on my experience at my former firm, and my partner's small commercial work. Strategically this was an error for me. If I had worked on larger projects before leaving the firm in Chicago, I think the experience would have helped us obtain work in the commercial world sooner.

I have had my own firm since 1990, and now have 9 (7 women) employees. We do residential and commercial work.

My goal in architecture has always been to do work that would be recognized and published, and to work with clients that really appreciate the process and the result. At the same time I have given lots of time to the A.I.A. because I think that women are not represented there enough, and the profession is not very inclusive of any minorities. The American Institute of Architects probably does more for firms than for individuals but even today struggles in its efforts to help small firms.

What has been interesting is to discover about my clients is that they are completely supportive of the idea that as a woman I can be a good or even better architect than some of my male counterparts. I have a few particularly supportive male clients who have practically handed me a job that was much larger than anything I had ever done before and knew that I could do it, including a 56 story residential highrise.

I am also married to an architect but we do not practice together, intentionally. He has his own firm also — a 40 person firm in Chicago. He has been a supporter as well, and some of my clients have come through his commercial connections to my more residential firm.

I think that the difficulties have been outweighed by the sense of accomplishment and enjoyment I have in this profession, which is not an easy one for either sex. I have found the most discrimination in the construction area, where we have found an unbelievable number of times that men do not like to listen to women tell them what to do. Even at my present age and experience I am dealing with a contractor today, not of my choosing, who would not follow the drawings or do the required paperwork until a mediator was brought in. Unfortunately the condo board for this job also would not fire this contractor, even after it was clear that the firm was unethical and dishonest, and we recommend that they do so.

Since I have had my own firm, the progression of jobs that have occurred has been uphill, but there were nights when I would come home in tears, saying "if I have to do another kitchen I will leave this profession."

There has always been a prejudice that women in the profession are better at interiors, which at first I railed against. After my first job in Chicago I didn't really want to do interiors, but with another woman in my firm, we have now opened a separate interiors firm, because keeping that control over the whole project is so much better, and I don't think that interiors are less important than the architecture anymore. I have come to the conclusion that the design of buildings is one long continuum and the more input we have from site design to interiors and furniture the better we can make it.

LETTER NO. 56
January 10, 2005
Midwest

I apologize for this tardy response to your letter of last November. While at Washington University I often received mail addressed to Ms. Constantine (rhymes with Clementine?) so I am not entirely surprised with yours! Unfortunately I am male and cannot contribute directly to your thoughtful project, which I applaud.

However, I served the School of Architecture at Washington University as its Dean for twenty years beginning in 1973. A treasured accomplishment of my leadership was the shift of the demography of the School in favor of substantial female enrollment. As far back as 1973 two female graduate students came to my office to share their discomfort of studying in a male dominated environment. Eventually we ended up organizing the first-ever national conference on the issue. Well-attended and organized the "Women in Architecture" 1974 conference, which you might remember, identified the School as a friendly and supportive environment and enabled the rapid increase of female undergraduate and graduate enrollments, which during the last several years of my Deanship had reached a stable 45%. The two then graduate students were Maggie Sedlis of New York and Hannah Roth of St. Louis, whom you might have possibly contacted during your earlier research.

I am also proud of the fact that by the time of my retirement the School was ready for its first female Dean and tenured faculty Cynthia Weese. If you have not contacted Cindy as yet about your project you may want to do it soon because she has announced her retirement at the end of this coming June.

I hope that the above is of some assistance to you and your project.

Best wishes for the success of your project and for a peaceful and creative New Year.

Constance Spencer at Atkins Architect: Gana Office Building, Toronto, Ontario, 1989. photo: courtesy, C. Spencer.

Constance Spencer at Atkins Architect: Greystone Golf Club, Milton, Ontario, 1991.
photo: courtesy, C. Spencer.

Constance Spencer at Spencer Architect / Hawkins Kibler / Charles McLarty:
VanLandingham Estate Conference Center, Charlotte, North Carolina, 2005.
photo: courtesy, C. Spencer.

Maria Elizabeth Cole, project designer at Davis Partnership Architects:
Biotechnology Laboratory renovation of industrial warehouse, Boulder, Colorado,
1992. photo: courtesy, M. E. Cole.

Maria Elizabeth Cole in collaboration with Andrew Moss: 456 House for Urban Infill, Denver, Colorado, 1999. photo: courtesy, M. E. Cole.

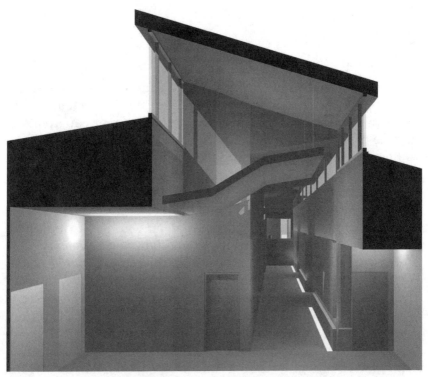

Maria Elizabeth Cole, project architect at Davis Partnership Architects: Anchor
Center for Blind Children, Stapleton Redevelopment, Denver, Colorado, 2007.
image: courtesy, M. E. Cole.

INQUIRY LETTERS — 1972 & 2004

Cambridge, MA
1972

I am doing research on Women in Architecture in the United States. This study includes women's contributions to architecture from the Indians, through early American architecture, to contemporary times. It is a most important subject and will be developed into a book.

For these reasons I wish to know about as many women architects as possible. Therefore, I am writing to you, one of the few women trained for this profession.

Hopefully I am not imposing upon you, but I would like very much to know more about you and how you have used your professional training. It is indeed important to such a study on Women in Architecture. Some of the questions I have in mind are as follows: What factors in your life led you to architecture? Where did you receive your professional training? Have you practiced your profession? If you have not practiced architecture, what were some of the reasons? What types of projects and what phases (design, working drawings, supervision, etc.) of the projects have you done? Have you been subjected to discrimination in salary, job promotions, etc. due to your sex? What are some of your goals in architecture?

I would like very much to hear from you, to hear all of your opinions and comments on this subject. Please don't feel limited to the few questions in the above paragraph. I would greatly appreciate your taking the time to answer.

Sincerely yours,

Doris Cole
Architect

COLE AND GOYETTE
Architects and Planners Inc.

955 Massachusetts Avenue
Cambridge, MA 02139
Tel. 617-491-5662
Fax. 617-492-0856
E-Mail: colegoyette@earthlink.net

November 2004

Dear Colleague:

We received a Boston Society of Architects (BSA) Research Grant for our project entitled, "Voices From the Past: Letters from 1970s Women Architects." As part of this research, we want to compare the views and experiences of past and current women architects.

In the process of conducting research for the first book on the history of women in architecture in 1973, Doris sent out an inquiry letter throughout the country asking women architects to comment on their lives, education, profession, and goals. Their candid responses were fascinating, touching, and inspiring.

We are now interested in receiving contemporary observations from current women architects. Our goal is to produce a unique collection of personal observations and reflections on the profession. All response letters, old and new, will be carefully edited to maintain confidentiality and anonymity. The results of our research will be presented in the form of a monograph to the Boston Society of Architects.

A copy of Doris' original 1972 inquiry letter is attached. Your comments and opinions would be greatly appreciated. We would very much like to hear from you by mail at the above address, or by email at colegoyette@earthlink.net. Thank you for taking the time to do this.

Sincerely yours,

Doris Cole, FAIA   Jason Knutson, AIA

LIST OF RESPONDENTS TO INQUIRY LETTERS

Roula Alakiotou, FAIA
Sari Berlin, AIA, NCARB
Amy B. Bonner
Sheila de Bretteville
Velma Chadwick
Elizabeth Coit, FAIA
Maria Cole, AIA
Margaret Courtney
Barbara J. Durand
Cynthia Faw, AIA, LEEDTM
Freda Gilfillan, RA
L. Jane Hastings, FAIA
Edith Jacobsen, AIA
Diane Legge Kemp, FAIA, ALSA
Julia Maser, AIA
Constance Michaelides, FAIA
Marilys Nepomechie, FAIA
Eve Nesom
Emily V. Obst, AIA
Joan C. Parker
Charlotte M. Parmely
Elizabeth G. Pattee, FASLA, AIA
Josephine E. Powers, AIA
Kathryn Quinn, AIA
Catherine Rands, AIA
Lucille Raport, AIA
Dorothea B. Rathbone
Sylvia Reay, AIA
Lutah Maria Riggs, AIA
Evelyn Rorex, AIA
Lorraine Rudoff, RA
Viola H. Russell
Charlotte V. Sape
A. Carol Sanford
Linda Searl, FAIA
Martha Seng, AIA

Lorene Lamar Shannon, AIA
Barbara W. Siemens, AIA
Mary Bardwick Sisson, RA
Laurie Smith, RA
Onny B. Smith, AIA
Jeane Brown Spear, AIA
Constance Spencer, RA
Sally Bould Stan
Mary Steinmesch, RA
Rachel Sutton
Betty Tarris (by C.V.Tarris)
Ellen Koger Taylor, AIA
Anne Tennent, RIBA, AIA
Reba Thompson
Beverley Thorne, RA
Marie C. Turner
Marilyn M. Urmston, RA
Marie L. Vanderbury, RA
Margaret Van Pelt Vilas, AIA
Bertha Yerex Whitman, RA
Constance Williams
Beverly Willis, FAIA
Zelma Wilson, AIA
Anita Jesse Winston, AIA
Marion Benjamin Woodbury
Marion Sims Wyeth
Edith Yang, AIA
Jeanne Young, AIA
Theresa H. Yuen, AIA
Kathryn Harris Zobel

AUTHOR'S BIOGRAPHY

Doris Cole is a licensed architect and author of several books and numerous essays on architecture. Her previous books include *Eleanor Raymond, Architect*; *From Tipi to Skyscraper: A History of Women in Architecture; The Lady Architects: Howe, Manning and Almy* 1893–1937, and *School Treasures: Architecture of Historic Boston Schools*. She has contributed essays to *Pilgrims and Pioneers: New England Women in the Arts* and *Women in American Architecture: A Historic and Contemporary Perspective*. She is president of Cole and Goyette, Architects and Planners Inc., in Cambridge, Massachusetts. The firm was founded by Doris Cole and Hal Goyette in 1981 and has won numerous awards for their educational, commercial, and residential buildings. In 1994, Ms. Cole was named a Fellow of the American Institute of Architects for her professional achievements. She received the A. B. cum laude from Radcliffe College in 1959 and the Master of Architecture from Harvard University Graduate School of Design in 1963. Doris Cole was born in Chicago, Illinois and grew up in Grand Rapids, Michigan.